Guillermo Maldonado is one of the c [barcode: W9-AZW-417] twenty-first century. His insights int[o] supernatural kingdom of God on earth in our modern times are contagious. His book is destined to become a modern classic.

—*Dr. Myles Munroe*
President and Founder, Bahamas Faith Ministries
International, Nassau, Bahamas

Pastor Maldonado has a worldwide ministry specializing in the miraculous. His book contains great revelation knowledge. I have seen Pastor Maldonado's ministry inside and out, and I like the fruit of both.

—*Marilyn Hickey*
President, Marilyn Hickey Ministries, Englewood, Colorado

Pastor Guillermo Maldonado is a dynamic leader of a vibrant ministry. I believe God has raised him up at this time to reach not only the Hispanic population in the United States but also all nations around the world.

—*Dr. Mark Rutland*
President, Oral Roberts University, Tulsa, Oklahoma

Guillermo Maldonado is one of the most eminent Christian leaders on the planet. He is an influencer of influencers, a brilliant orator, a quintessential teacher, and a loving pastor.

—*Mark J. Chironna, Ph.D.*
Bishop, The Master's Touch International Church,
Orlando, Florida

Pastor Maldonado's heart for people and his family, and his family's *complete* devotion to announcing God's presence and power at all times, are completely pure and unrelenting.

—*Darlene Zschech*
Praise and worship artist

Pastor Maldonado is a man who has shared in my journey and recognizes the impact Jesus Christ has had on the lives of individuals like me. If you are looking for someone to help bridge your spiritual gap, Pastor Maldonado is the man to do so. I am proud to call him a friend.

—*Governor Rick Scott*
Florida

In *How to Walk in the Supernatural Power of God*, readers will find a source of spiritual enrichment and an invitation to know, in the words of the author, a "supernatural, almighty God who still performs miracles."

—*Alvaro Uribe Vélez*
Former President (2002–2010), Colombia

Guillermo Maldonado is a leader with great vision and faith. There is a great awakening coming to the nations of the earth with signs, wonders, and miracles, and Maldonado is on the forefront of it.

—*Cindy Jacobs*
Co-founder, Generals International, Dallas, Texas

When you sit under the mantle of Guillermo Maldonado, you receive healing and a word from the Lord, as well as encouragement. As an author, he takes readers into the essence of what the ministry is meant to be, but, most of all, he takes them into the presence of God.

—*Kimberly Daniels*
Founder, Kimberly Daniels Ministries International,
Jacksonville, Florida

Pastor Guillermo Maldonado is the most dynamic leader I have ever met! His ministry emphasizes power, spiritual maturity, and integrity. It has always impressed me how he can do all things with such excellence.

—*Steven Strang*
Founder and editor, *Charisma* magazine

Pastor Maldonado is truly an inspiring spiritual leader. I am honored by his friendship and guidance and inspired by his leadership and willingness to always put others before him.

—*Mario Diaz-Balart*
U.S. Representative, Florida's 21st District

Guillermo Maldonado is leaving a legacy to those who want to learn more about how to live in continuous revival. In *How to Walk in the Supernatural Power of God*, he makes every effort to place the miracle power of God within everyone's reach.

—*Cash Luna*
Pastor, Casa de Dios, Guatemala City, Guatemala

Guillermo's teachings and writings cover the fundamentals of the Christian faith.

—*Bill Hamon*
Founder and Bishop, Christian International Ministries Network

Pastor Guillermo Maldonado stands today as one of the leading voices in the kingdom of God and the preeminent forerunner of a biblical apostolic and prophetic movement with signs, wonders, and miracles following.

—*Rev. Samuel Rodriguez*
President, National Hispanic Christian Leadership Conference

The compelling fact of Guillermo Maldonado's life is that he has taken the words of Jesus literally: *"Go therefore and make disciples of all the nations"* (Matthew 28:19). If your desire is to be a disciple-maker, I encourage you to embrace Pastor Maldonado and his teaching.

—*Rich Wilkerson*
Pastor, Trinity Church, Miami, Florida

Maldonado has made significant contributions to the kingdom of God, changing the spiritual climate with his empowering teachings, which have forever changed the lives of thousands in this country and abroad. As a leader, he has skills and gifting of an extremely high caliber.

—*Tudor Bismark*
Bishop, New Life Covenant Church, Harare, Zimbabwe

In Guillermo Maldonado, the Lord has found a man after His own heart who is dedicated to fulfilling the will of God. He is a pioneer who displays God's power to a generation that desperately needs it.

—**Hank Kunneman**
Pastor, Lord of Hosts Church/One Voice Ministries,
Omaha, Nebraska

By his words and by his example, my dear friend Guillermo Maldonado has touched the souls and revived the faith of many men and women around the world. He is a source of inspiration for those who already walk in our Lord's path and a transforming hand for those who are close to the Creator.

—**Elías Antonio Saca González**
Former President (2004–2009), El Savador

Pastor Guillermo Maldonado is an outstanding pastor, church planter, visionary, and mentor to other church leaders. Both in the pulpit and through the power of his pen, Pastor Maldonado is a truly successful Christian leader, possessing both natural and spiritual gifts.

—**Marcus Lamb**
President and CEO, Daystar Television Network

Guillermo Maldonado is a humble man with huge, childlike faith. Through his ministry, God has performed many outstanding miracles. He is a loving pastor to his people, an excellent husband and father to his family, and a dedicated spiritual father to his flock.

—**Alan Vincent**
Cofounder, Outpouring Ministries, San Antonio, Texas

Maldonado is a spearhead in the prophetic reform that God is establishing at this time. With valor and faith, he has destroyed the spirit of conformity that has kept many ministries stagnant.

—**Wanda Rolón**
La Primera Cristiana La Senda Antigua, Toa Alta, Puerto Rico

Pastor, teacher, preacher, author, composer, ambassador, statesman, and friend—this is who Guillermo Maldonado is. The ministry and message of this dynamic kingdom-builder are changing the world we live in by impacting thousands of lives each year. If you read his words carefully, they will change you, too!

—*Paul Wilbur*
Recording artist, Integrity Music

Guillermo Maldonado has the gift of communication and the ability to transmit the Word of God in a manner that is absolutely unique. He is also the personification of service, always thinking of others, working for others, and serving our community and the nation. It is my honor to call him my friend.

—*Lincoln Diaz-Balart*
Former U.S. Representative (1993–2011), Florida's 21st District

The heart of Guillermo Maldonado's ministry is to get people saved, confirmed, trained, and discipled. In my forty-plus years of ministry and service unto the Lord Jesus Christ, I can truly say that Maldonado is the visual manifestation of the parable of the mustard seed that grew into a great tree.

—*Dr. Ronald E. Short*
Founder, Ronald Short Ministry

I call Guillermo Maldonado my friend and a man for whom I have the greatest respect. In his ministry, I see Jesus in the now, and the government of God is demonstrated in everything he says and does.

—*Dr. Renny McLean*
Global Glory Ministries, Dallas, Texas

Guillermo Maldonado is on the cutting edge of ministry, and his book blesses the body of Christ. He has a great hunger to see the souls of men and women saved by God's power!

—*R. J. Washington*
Pastor, Titus Harvest Dome Spectrum Church
Jacksonville, Florida

Guillermo Maldonado is a man whom God has raised to manifest His glory and heaven's supernatural power on earth. It is a normal occurrence to hear him preach and, later, to see a flow of creative miracles take place that impact even the minds of unbelievers.

—*Eduardo Cañas Estrada*
Pastor, Iglesia Comunidad Cristiana Manantial de Vida
Eterna, Bogotá, Colombia

How to Walk in the

Supernatural

POWER

of GOD

GUILLERMO MALDONADO

WHITAKER
HOUSE

HOW TO WALK IN THE SUPERNATURAL POWER OF GOD:
EXPERIENCE SIGNS, WONDERS, AND MIRACLES NOW

Guillermo Maldonado
13651 S.W. 143rd Ct., #101
Miami, FL 33186
www.ERJPub.org

ISBN: 978-1-60374-278-8
Printed in the United States of America
© 2011 by Guillermo Maldonado

Whitaker House
1030 Hunt Valley Circle
New Kensington, PA 15068
www.whitakerhouse.com

Library of Congress Cataloging-in-Publication Data

Maldonado, Guillermo.
  How to walk in the supernatural power of God / Guillermo Maldonado.
      p. cm.
  ISBN 978-1-60374-278-8 (trade pbk. : alk. paper) 1. Miracles. 2. Christian life—Pentecostal authors. I. Title.
  BT97.3.M35 2011
  234'.13—dc22
                              2011002517

3 4 5 6 7 8 9 10 11 12 **UJ** 18 17 16 15 14 13 12 11

Acknowledgments

I take this opportunity to express my gratitude and to honor several men and women who have been a great blessing to me, not only in the past but also in the present. In one way or another, they have inspired me in the ministry by releasing the prophetic word over me and by their continuous prayers. Some have been "fathers in the faith" to me. Others have been mentors in a specific area of my life and ministry. Others are my personal friends, just like Paul and Barnabas. Still others are my spiritual children, as Timothy was to Paul. At all times, they have supported and stood by me.

The Word teaches us to honor those who deserve to be honored, and this is one way I would like to recognize their individual support.

The measure of faith God has given them has been of great help to me. It has strengthened and enriched me. These individuals have encouraged me to seek newer and deeper territories in God and a greater level of growth in His glory, anointing, and power. They have been role models in my life and have inspired me during the past two decades in ministry. When the ministry experienced times of great need, they gave me the prophetic word. During difficult times, they served me and my family. These things touched my heart so deeply that today I take this opportunity to publicly thank them. All of them have been a great blessing to me, in my personal life, as well as in the pulpit. I have learned much from watching how they carry on in their personal lives and from their integrity. Many of them have shared important revelations that inspired me and have helped me to write this book.

First, I thank my beloved wife, Ana, for her continued support in prayer, and my sons, Bryan and Ronald, for their unconditional support. Also, Prophet Cindy Jacobs; Apostle Ronald Short; Apostle Alan Vincent; my spiritual father, Bishop Bill Hamon; Prophet Hank Kunneman; Prophet Cathy Lechner; Apostle Kim Daniels; Apostle Cash Luna; Dr. Marilyn Hickey; Pastor Charles Green; Dr. Richard Roberts; Bishop R.J. Washington; Prophet Kim Clement; Pastor Tommy Tenney; Dr. Myles Munroe; Dr. Rodney Howard Browne; Pastor Benny Hinn; Evangelist Roy Durman; T. L. Osborn; and Dr. Renny McLean. Also, my most sincere thanks to the pastors, prophets, and ministers, my spiritual children, for your support—for some have been with me since the onset of this ministry. My deepest gratitude to each of you. I honor you and bless you because you have been a permanent source of inspiration to me. Thank you.

—*Apostle Guillermo Maldonado*

Contents

1

The Revelation of a Supernatural God

As we witness the events taking place around the world, we begin to realize that biblical prophecies like this one are coming to pass. Both the frequency and severity of "natural disasters," such as earthquakes, hurricanes, and tsunamis, seem to be on the rise. Evil seems to be increasing, not decreasing, in society. Rebellion, wars, and rumors of war fill the evening newscasts. Hunger is a terrible problem, as nearly one billion of the world's people will go to bed hungry tonight. Financial crises are affecting countries around the globe where deceit, lies, insecurity, and fear abound. People are desperately looking for answers to these problems, but neither governments nor political leaders nor the religious system seems able to offer valid solutions. Sadly, religion has, for the most part, offered the world only a historic god—an "elder of days" who sits on his throne, waiting for the world to fail so he can punish it; a distant god who lacks both supernatural ability and an intimate relationship with mankind. Thankfully, this ineffectual god is not the real, living God of Scripture.

The fundamental purpose of this book is to give you the answers you need in order to live in victory, peace, and joy—even in a world that seems to be falling deeper and deeper into darkness with each passing day. Here, you will come face-to-face with a powerful and supernatural God—a God who works miracles like the ones He performed centuries ago, a God who hates sin but loves the sinner. The God you will discover in this book manifested that infinite love by sending His one and only Son to earth as a sign of His unrelenting love for us. This is the same God who performed healings, miracles, signs, and wonders in the Old Testament, the same God who continued to perform them through the early church during the time of the apostles, and the same God who continues to perform those same miracles, signs, and wonders through His body—all those who put their trust in Him. He has given us supernatural power to live in victory. Without the ingredient of His supernatural power, it is impossible to overcome tribulation, sickness, and any other adverse circumstances that rise against us.

A Hunger for the Supernatural

Today, we see a generation filled with unanswered questions. They hunger and thirst for God. Their thirst has not been satiated because religion does not offer valid answers. Most of them want to have a real relationship with the living God and yearn to be used by Him to manifest His supernatural power on earth.

The world seeks answers to the following questions:

- Does God continue to perform miracles today?
- What does a life of miracles do for us?
- Can Christianity be considered relevant if it operates without miracles?
- What makes the Christian life more than just another religion or philosophy?
- Do we need the miracles mentioned in the Bible today?
- What makes a Christian credible?
- What proof can we offer people that Jesus lives, and that He is not just another good teacher or wise guru?
- Can rituals, rules, or regulations change people?
- Through whom does God perform miracles?
- Can anyone be the recipient of a miracle?

All of these questions will be answered as you read this book. In addition to getting to know a supernatural and powerful God who continues to perform miracles, you will also come to learn about the complete work of Jesus at the cross, and how, through the cross, He fully provided for every need you might face. You will discover that the cross is the only source of the supernatural. You will learn how to live a life of faith in the midst of a dangerous and uncertain world. You will understand how to walk in the anointing and how to transition into walking in God's glory. And you will learn how to receive your miracle and what to do so that God may use you to perform miracles that will bless other people. You will know how to walk in the supernatural power of God. As you read this book, you may even find yourself receiving healing and experiencing creative miracles. If you are missing an organ, God can create a new one within you, just as He did in the people whose testimonies you will read. You may receive financial miracles or deliverance in your mind and emotions. God will impart revelation, activation, and transformation to you so that you may finally become one who is chosen by Him to manifest His power wherever you go. You will be enabled to testify to Jesus, pray for the sick, cast out demons, and work miracles as you carry out the Great Commission by taking the gospel into the world, making disciples, and having dominion over the earth.

Dare to take this journey with me. With each chapter, you will come to know the supernatural, powerful, and immutable God for whom all things are possible, a God who can change and transform your life forever.

When we contemplate the greatness of God's creation, our finite imaginations cannot fathom His great power and love. Man has tried to know his Creator through intellectual means, but this has proven impossible because God can be known only through revelation. His intention was never to remain a mystery to His people. In fact, He has always desired for us to know Him intimately and to experience His attributes, strengths, and virtues. To reveal Himself as the supernatural and all-powerful God, He sent us His Holy Spirit. There is no other means by which we can know Him. God cannot be defined because no person has the mental ability to describe the infinite or the eternal. However, in this chapter, I will try to present some basic and uncomplicated information that will help you to understand Him in human terms.

Who Is God?

God is a spiritual, eternal, and immutable being with supernatural attributes and abilities. He dwells in the dimension of eternity—the spiritual realm—and manifests in visible form in the natural dimension.

Thus says the High and Lofty One who inhabits eternity.
(Isaiah 57:15)

The only way to know God is through revelation, but what is revelation? In Greek, the word for "revelation" is *apokalypsis*, which means "laying bare, making naked…a disclosure of truth, instruction concerning things before unknown." This expression is particularly used in understanding the spiritual realm.

Revelation

Revelation is the knowledge of God revealed to our spirits, and it is received by spiritually seeing, hearing, and perceiving. This process is referred to as "spiritual perception." Revelation allows you to suddenly understand something without the aid of the natural senses. This knowledge or understanding can be given only by the Holy Spirit, as in the case of Peter, who received the revelation that Jesus was the Messiah because the Father had revealed it to him through the Holy Spirit.

Flesh and blood has not revealed this to you, but My Father who is in heaven. (Matthew 16:17)

To receive revelation from God is to see as He sees, to hear as He hears, and to perceive as He perceives.

Revelation includes knowing things you otherwise would not know, seeing things that have yet to occur, and perceiving things without prior knowledge. It is the mind of God revealed so that mankind can exercise dominion over time, space, and matter.

In Western culture, intellectual formation has overtaken divine revelation, pushing the latter into second-place status. Thus, we are trained to reject anything and everything that makes no sense or that cannot be explained according to human understanding.

Mankind criticizes everything he cannot create or understand.

In the absence of progressive divine revelation, people tend to turn to formal, natural intellectual education, much of which serves to discredit faith. Intellectual knowledge has its rightful place in society, but it is a poor substitute for spiritual knowledge.

Who Is the Source of Revealed Knowledge?

The Source of all revelation is the Holy Spirit. He is the only channel that gives us access to God's revealed wisdom or knowledge. The Holy Spirit hears what is said in heaven and repeats it to men and women on earth. We cannot know God without the help of the Holy Spirit. Theologians may *know* that a superior being exists, but that does not mean that they *know* Him personally. Many of them merely operate with information acquired through intellectual research, reasoning, mental processes, or the experiences of others.

How Did the Apostle Paul Handle Natural Knowledge?

However, we speak wisdom among those who are mature, yet not the wisdom of this age, nor of the rulers of this age, who are coming to nothing. But we speak the wisdom of God in a mystery, the hidden wisdom which God ordained before the ages for our glory.

(1 Corinthians 2:6–7)

Philosophy is a science based on a love of wisdom that is obtained from the natural environment. Therefore, when Paul mentioned *"the wisdom of this age,"* he was referring to prominent Greek philosophy—he had lived in Greece for two years. However, while in Athens, when Paul spoke on wisdom, he failed to effectively preach the gospel, and, after those two years, he had not planted a single church there. Upon his return to the church in Corinth, he emphatically expressed that he had returned in God's power and not in human wisdom. Paul, then, understood that human wisdom and philosophy were incapable of producing the supernatural power required to preach the gospel or to manifest God's power.

God's Wisdom

I became a minister according to the stewardship from God which was given to me for you, to fulfill the word of God, the mystery which has been hidden from ages and from generations, but now has been revealed to His saints. To them God willed to make known what are the riches of the glory of this mystery among the Gentiles: which is Christ in you, the hope of glory.

(Colossians 1:25–27)

Why search for revelation in the world when all the deep treasures of wisdom can be found in Christ?

The wisdom of our Lord Jesus Christ is to share His secrets through the cross.

Eye has not seen, nor ear heard, nor have entered into the heart of man the things which God has prepared for those who love Him. (1 Corinthians 2:9)

The natural senses alone cannot perceive the revealed wisdom or knowledge of God. However, these mysteries have already been revealed through the Holy Spirit.

But God has revealed them to us through His Spirit. For the Spirit searches all things, yes, the deep things of God. For what man knows the things of a man except the spirit of the man which is in him? Even so no one knows the things of God except the Spirit of God. (1 Corinthians 2:10–11)

This is an inviolable truth. The human mind is not able to know everything that is in man; only the Holy Spirit knows all things. Consequently, the only One who can reveal God is the Spirit of God, the administrator of the grace of Jesus on earth. It is surprising to see Christians turning to philosophy, psychology, and psychiatry to try to resolve their problems. These disciplines genuinely try to help people but fail to utilize the power of God to change and transform mankind. Therefore, it is useless to apply biblical terms while pursuing such man-made methods.

The truth of the Bible can be properly expressed only by using the language of the Bible.

Four Truths that Can Be Known Only through Revelation:

- The nature of God
- The nature of man

- The origin of man
- The origin of life

These truths cannot be fully discovered through scientific, natural, psychological, psychiatric, or philosophical means. If we choose to reject the concept of divine revelation, we will never fully understand these truths, and we will continue to live in confusion and deception. Scientists and avid students seek to use only mental processes and the systematic collection of information acquired through the natural senses. Within such limitations, they have no choice but to deny God because their workable knowledge does not allow them to accept Him. They often don't know where their knowledge comes from and steadfastly believe that the world exists because matter somehow created itself. Sensory knowledge has become their primary source of wisdom, but this knowledge cannot explain the origin of creation or the beginning of matter, and it lacks valid answers to the great "whys" of humanity. Scientists have developed diverse theories on the origin of life and the nature of God. They have written countless volumes on the subject, all derived from the same restrictive sources that are supplied by human senses and reasoning, as well as the limitations of creatures that fail to acknowledge their Creator. Formal education has not contributed to the faith of millions of young people. They are raised and trained to recognize and accept only that which they can see, feel, decipher, and explain with their physical senses and intellect.

The only way to know God and to relate to His supernatural and invisible realm is by faith.

Many theologians and philosophers speculate about the nature of God. They seek to understand Him through logic but fail in their attempts. Plato tried to analyze God and concluded that He does not exist. Aristotle also concluded that God is not real. Many other scientists and theologians have reasoned the same, but this is because they failed to understand that God can be known and understood only by faith and revelation.

God is always the One who chooses to reveal Himself to us, and the One who has provided the way. Thus, we must depend solely on Him. If God had not chosen to reveal Himself, we never would have known Him.

God's Methods of Revelation

God cannot reveal Himself to those who lack the desire to know Him, or to those who choose not to have a relationship with Him. For this reason, Jesus hid the mysteries of the kingdom from the religious leaders of His time and said, *"Do not... cast your pearls before swine"* (Matthew 7:6). Jesus spoke in parables precisely to keep certain mysteries hidden from those who had no intention of knowing God, and from those who sought such knowledge only as ammunition for debate rather than as an authentic experience.

God's Revelation Depends On:

- God's time
- God's will

Many believers, leaders, and godly men have no idea what God is saying or doing in their personal lives, in the body of Christ, or in the world precisely because they lack revelation. God said that in the last days, knowledge would increase (see Daniel 12:3–4) because it is His will to fill the earth with His glory (see Numbers 14:21). I believe that we are living in those last days, days in which the manifestation of His glory will be evident everywhere.

Revealed knowledge is closely linked to Christ's coming.

Your faith will be strongest in the area in which you have the greatest revealed knowledge from God. Likewise, your faith will be weakest where you lack revelation or have little of it.

The enemy establishes a stronghold where God's knowledge and revelation do not exist.

What Are the Two Realms that Exist?

- The natural realm
- The supernatural realm

What is the natural realm? It is the dimension that is subject to the laws of time, space, and matter, a dimension that can be accessed only through the physical senses.

What is the supernatural realm? It is the dimension that operates above natural laws. It is the spiritual realm—permanent, invisible, and eternal—located outside of time. It exercises dominion over the natural realm. The spiritual realm can be accessed only by faith.

We do not look at the things which are seen, but at the things which are not seen. For the things which are seen are temporary, but the things which are not seen are eternal. (2 Corinthians 4:18)

During a supernatural service at our church, miracles, healings, salvations, and transformations occur. Manifestations of the Holy Spirit also occur, including signs, wonders, unexpected cancellations of debts, financial miracles, deliverances from demons, and much more.

Now, let us begin to understand the invisible, eternal, and omnipotent God, and let me describe what can occur at what we at our church call a Healing and Miracle Service. For many who attend these services, it may be their last opportunity for life and health. In many cases, science has reached its limit and is unable to provide a solution to their health problems. They come with the desire to experience God's supernatural power.

On one particular day, while I was praying at home, God specifically told me that He was going to heal the blind. During our next Healing and Miracle Service, I called for the sick and afflicted to come forward. Among them was a woman who had been blind in her left eye since birth. Doctors had declared this woman's condition incurable and told her that she should settle for having sight in only her right eye. As I prayed and declared God's Word over the woman, she began to feel an intense heat within her body. At that moment, the Holy Spirit reminded her of the verse that says, *"The kingdom of heaven suffers violence, and the violent take it by force"* (Matthew 11:12). Seizing that verse, she chose to believe God, claimed His promises, and forcefully took possession of her healing. The audience was astonished to hear me ask her to do what she had been unable to do before the service. I asked her to focus all of her attention on seeing through her left eye. To her surprise, she found that she could see through both eyes! At first, all she saw were blurry images, but, in time, her vision continued to clear up until everything became perfectly visible. God had healed her! He had restored her left eye! He had returned what the devil had stolen from her at birth: her vision! God's supernatural power had given her a creative miracle. What had been impossible by medical and scientific means, God had done in one instant!

What did we do that day? We activated the supernatural power of God, and the miracles started to flow. Science could not heal this woman, but God did it instantly!

Throughout Scripture, we learn of a God who operates in a supernatural way, who dwells outside of time, who is able to interrupt time, space, and matter if He so desires. This is what we call a "miracle." I define a *miracle* as "the supernatural intervention of God that interrupts the normal course of the natural life." When He removes His finger, natural time resumes once again. Every day, we urgently need God to interrupt our daily existence so we can see His divine manifestations and miracles. He is a God of miracles. And we see this truth in the following examples from Scripture.

God Stops the Sun

Then Joshua...said in the sight of Israel: "Sun, stand still over Gibeon; and Moon, in the Valley of Aijalon." So the sun stood still, and the moon stopped, till the people had revenge upon their enemies. (Joshua 10:12–13)

God is able to stop the clock at any moment. When He did it with Joshua, Scripture says that the sun stopped. Of course, because of discoveries in astronomy, we now know that the earth orbits the sun, not the other way around. When Joshua gave the order, therefore, it was actually the earth that stood still, not the sun. In addition to orbiting the sun, the earth rotates on its axis, making a complete turn every twenty-four hours at a speed close to one thousand miles per hour. This rotation is what produces night and day, sunrise and sunset. With this in mind, why did Joshua order the sun to stop if it is the earth that is in orbit? Joshua was simply speaking from his point of view. If you are in a moving car, and you see a person who is standing on the next corner, it might seem as though the person is approaching you, when, in truth, it is your car that is approaching the person. The most incredible aspect of this miracle is that the earth actually did stand still! It stopped rotating without being destroyed. We cannot limit God. He is supernatural and all-powerful. He has complete and total dominion over nature.

In the Old Testament, God showed Himself to be a supernatural God of miracles:

- At the Tower of Babel, God divided the people by giving them new languages (see Genesis 11:5–8);

- At Sodom and Gomorrah, God destroyed entire cities with fire from heaven (see Genesis 19:24–25);

- God saved Moses from Pharaoh's plot to kill Israel's first-born sons (see Exodus 12);

- In the desert, God spoke to Moses from a bush that burned without being consumed (see Exodus 3);

- In Egypt, God turned Aaron's rod into a serpent (see Exodus 7:10–12), turned the Nile River into blood (see Exodus 7:14–24), and caused plagues of frogs, lice, flies, boils, and locusts (see Exodus 7–10);

- God parted the Red Sea and delivered Israel out of Egypt and slavery (see Exodus 13:17–14:29);

- In the wilderness, God caused manna to descend from heaven every day (see Exodus 16:1–24), sent quail for them to eat (see Numbers 11:31–32), and drew water from a rock (see Exodus 17:6; Number 20:8–12);

- He caused earthquakes to defeat and drive off the Philistines (see 1 Samuel 14:15);

- He destroyed the walls of Jericho (see Joshua 6);

- He caused an axe head to float on water (see 2 Kings 6:6);

- He gave Samson the strength to kill a lion and tear down the columns of the Philistines with his hands (see Judges 14:5–6; 16:21–30);

- He gave Abraham and his sterile wife, Sarah, a son in their old age (see Genesis 21:1–3);

- He enabled a young shepherd named David to kill a giant named Goliath with only a sling and a stone (see 1 Samuel 17);

- He fed the widow of Zarephath with the multiplication of oil and flour (see 1 Kings 17:8–15);

- He caused a donkey to speak (see Numbers 22–24);

- He consumed Elijah's sacrifice on Mount Carmel (see 1 Kings 18:16–46);

- He commanded rain to fall after a drought (see 1 Kings 18:16–46);

- He healed Naaman through His prophet (see 2 Kings 5:1–19);

- He raised a man from death when the man's body touched Elisha's bones (2 Kings 13:14, 20–21);
- He kept Shadrach, Meshach, and Abed-Nego safe and unharmed in a fiery furnace (see Daniel 3);
- He kept Daniel safe when the king placed him in a lions' den (see Daniel 6:10–23);
- He preserved the life of Jonah in the belly of a whale (see Jonah 1–2).

And these are but a few examples.

We also see a miracle when God sent His only Son, Jesus, to reveal the heavenly Father as a supernatural God, and when His Son performed spectacular miracles, such as when He:

- Turned water into wine (see John 2:1–11);
- Healed the ten lepers, a centurion's servant, a paralytic, Peter's mother-in-law, and a deaf-mute (see, for example, Luke 17:11–19; Matthew 8:5–13; Luke 5:17–26; Mark 1:29–39; 7:31–37);
- Straightened the back of the woman who had been bent for many years (see Luke 13:10–17);
- Healed the blind beggar by the pool (see Mark 10:46–52);
- Restored sight to one who was blind from birth (see John 9:1–25);
- Raised the son of the widow of Nain from the dead (see Luke 7:11–17);
- Delivered the daughter of the Syro-Phoenician woman (see Mark 7:24–30);
- Raised Lazarus three days after his death (see John 11:1–27);
- Multiplied the bread and the fish and fed five thousand people (see Mark 6:30–44);
- Walked on water (see Matthew 14:22–33);
- Provided money from the mouth of a fish (see Matthew 17:24–27);

- Cursed the fig tree, causing it to dry up (see Matthew 21:18–21);
- And delivered a demon-possessed man (see Mark 5:1–20).

Most of all, we see it when Jesus surrendered to the cross, descended into hell, took the keys of death from Satan, and was bodily raised from the dead before ascending to heaven and sending us His Holy Spirit. In addition, we see it in the miracles that took place in the early church. And we continue to marvel at the miracles, signs, and wonders God performs in the church today.

The Two Sources of Supernatural Power

- God
- Satan

Any supernatural power that does not come from God is from Satan. Therefore, we must be alert to avoid being deceived. Man was created to enjoy and exercise God's supernatural power.

Then God said, "Let Us make man in Our image, according to Our likeness; let them have dominion over the fish of the sea, over the birds of the air, and over the cattle, over all the earth and over every creeping thing that creeps on the earth." (Genesis 1:26)

Man was created with supernatural power to exercise dominion and lordship on the earth. He was not created to trust solely in his natural abilities, mind, reasoning, or any other source of sensorial knowledge offered by the world. Man was created to walk in the supernatural power of God.

The Supernatural God Revealed Himself through Jesus

And Peter answered [Jesus] and said, "Lord, if it is You, command me to come to You on the water." So [Jesus] said, "Come." And when Peter had come down out of the boat, he walked on the water to go to Jesus.

(Matthew 14:28–29)

Walking on water was one of Jesus' most awesome miracles. When Peter saw Him, he said he wanted to do the same thing, and Jesus answered, *"Come."* As soon as Peter started to walk on the water, however, he felt the strong wind and focused on the storm, took his eyes off of Jesus, and began to sink. Notice that Jesus did not rebuke Peter for wanting to walk on water, too. On the contrary, Jesus encouraged Peter to do it. Why did Peter want to walk on water? What was his motive? Peter left the safety of the boat because he was prompted by the instinctual need for supernatural power that resides in man, the desire to cross over the line from the natural into the supernatural. Unfortunately, that same instinctual need has led many men away from God and toward destructive supernatural options, such as magic, witchcraft, diabolical games, false religions, satanic sects, idolatry, and much more.

If we observe men and women today, we will notice that some rely solely on their natural abilities, trusting only in science, technology, mathematics, philosophy, logic, and other branches of human intellect and understanding. Others opt for witchcraft or other ungodly supernatural powers. Many fail to realize that their choices lead to idolatry and dissatisfaction. For this reason, God is raising a new generation with the audacity to leave the boat, "walk on the water," and do miracles in His name. This new generation wants more because God has placed that desire within them.

Today's Generation

When this generation goes to church looking for God's supernatural power, most do not find it because many churches preach a Jesus who is dead and historic—a man from Sunday school stories. To these people, the powerful, supernatural, real, living, raised-from-the-dead Jesus remains a complete stranger. As a result, when people witness a miracle today, they are unable to believe it because they lack the revelation of the true Christ. Due to this lack of power in the church, many young people have returned to the world in search of another source of power—that of the devil.

Most young adults have never witnessed or heard about God's supernatural power due to their unstable faith founded on human wisdom rather than on the revelation of Jesus. Today, many seek "supernatural" power by other means, including drugs, alcohol, divination, and witchcraft. Their desire for power is good, but the way they are trying to satisfy this desire is evil. Therefore, they become easy targets for the devil, who seeks to destroy them.

Let us now explore some testimonies of God's supernatural power for this generation.

A young adult in our church decided to go to the gas station and buy some coffee during his lunch hour. In front of the line was a very attractive lady who gave the impression of being wealthy. Immediately, the Holy Spirit showed this young man that the woman needed help, so he approached her and said, "I have a word for you. Would you wait for me to pay for my coffee and then I'll share it with you?" She agreed. After he paid, they went outside, and the young man said, "I feel that you recently lost a loved one, perhaps a week ago." The lady was perplexed and answered, "Yes, my father died last week." Immediately, she began to cry. He felt such compassion for her that he said, "Your heavenly Father is watching you today, and He wants to become real to you, but only Jesus can bring you close to the Father." He then shared a few personal details about her private life, including her marital relationship. This young man had no idea what he was saying, so he knew that it was the Holy Spirit who was personally ministering to this woman. God was saying so much, in such clear detail, that the words affected her spirit. Anyone would have noticed the impact these words were making by the way she was receiving them. Finally, she raised her hands and, in front of everyone at the gas station, confessed Jesus as her

Lord and Savior and received the love of our heavenly Father as tears of joy fell down her cheeks. This is God's love!

In another demonstration of His great love for His people, God performed a creative miracle that greatly affected me and the multitudes gathered at a Healing and Miracle Crusade in Villa Hermosa, Mexico. After praying according to His Word, I declared healing for the people. Afterward, a man came up to give his testimony. He had been born deaf in one ear, and his doctors had discovered that he was missing the right auditory system; he didn't even have an orifice for the ear. In other words, his ear was completely sealed, with only a small trace of an external ear. When I declared God's Word, he felt a quick explosion take place on the side of his head, likened to a cork coming off a bottle, and he immediately began to hear out of the ear that had been sealed. God performed a creative miracle in Mexico! He created a new auditory system where there had been none. One of the doctors present examined him and declared that it was impossible for this man to hear without the orifice or the auditory system, which were necessary to transport the sound waves. God worked His perfect will, and this man returned home with perfect hearing in both his ears. Praise the Lord!

A few youths in our church showed us how the truth can transform the present reality.

One Thursday night, I was preaching on the subject of boldness. After receiving the Word, one of the youth ministers of our church dared to practice what he had heard during the message. So, after eating with a few of his friends at a restaurant in Miami, he decided to visit the bar next to the restaurant. That's right, a bar! The young minister and two of his friends entered the establishment, while the rest of the group stayed outside, where they talked to people about Jesus. He had seized that night's message and said, "I am going to win all those drunks for Jesus tonight." He began by sharing some words about science with the people in the bar, who were already drunk. Then, he shared the message of the gospel of the kingdom, and something incredible happened. Everyone in the bar repeated the Sinner's Prayer aloud. Through this testimony, we see that when we preach the gospel, the lost will be saved, and the atmosphere will also change. That's right. The atmosphere in that bar changed! How do I know this? Because, before long, it closed down. Today, it no longer exists! This is a clear demonstration that the Word of God never returns void! (See Isaiah 55:11.)

Enemies of the Supernatural God

1. Ignorance

Therefore my people have gone into captivity, because they have no knowledge. (Isaiah 5:13)

The devil hates revealed knowledge because it leads to deliverance. When people discover the truth, they are delivered, but when they lack knowledge, they are held captive in their ignorance.

2. Bad theology

Theology is the study of God through the mind and reason. When we study God with improper motivation, or without inspiration, illumination, and revelation from the Holy Spirit, theology becomes *carnal*—of a worldly intellect that is influenced more by the desires of the flesh than by the Spirit. However, it is good to clarify that there is a good theology, one that studies God with revelation from the Holy Spirit. I am blessed to be a graduate of Oral Roberts University, and, without fear of making a mistake, I believe it is one of the few universities in the world where God is studied under the inspiration and authority of the Holy Spirit. Having obtained my master's degree, I can now say that I know God on a more intimate level. What I have experienced in His presence has been much more intense and powerful. We need theology, but only that which comes by revelation imparted by the Holy Spirit.

3. Humanism

Humanism is the collection of philosophical ideas that elevate man to the highest position in terms of esteem. During the

Renaissance, reason and thought increased in value. Within the Christian realm, this was a good thing. However, modern humanism has become more and more secular. It rejects God and His supernatural power while positioning man essentially as a god. Humanism celebrates human reason and intellect alone, making it anti-God.

4. The "spirit of Jezebel," or witchcraft

The "spirit of Jezebel" refers to Queen Jezebel, one of the most evil persons in the Bible. After she married Ahab, the king of Israel, her controlling and domineering nature led the nation into worshipping false gods. (See 1 Kings 16:31.) She also ordered the extermination of all of God's prophets. (See 1 Kings 18:4, 13.) A reference to the spirit of Jezebel applies to anyone who acts in the same manner—engaging in immorality, idolatry, false teaching, and unrepentant sin.

> *O foolish Galatians! Who has bewitched you that you should not obey the truth...?* (Galatians 3:1)

The apostle Paul used the word *bewitched*, which means "to bring evil on one by feigning praise or an evil eye...to charm, to bewitch." In Paul's mind, witchcraft was blinding the people's understanding and keeping them from recognizing the redeeming work of Christ on the cross.

What opens the door to witchcraft? Rebellion, which consists of stirring up or subverting any authorities established by God. Rebellion replaces divine authority with an illegitimate one that is sustained by the spirit of witchcraft. Its purpose is to manipulate, control, intimidate, and dominate in order to nullify the supernatural power of the cross.

5. The carnal mind

The carnal mind is one that is based in this worldly reality. I want to clarify that it is not bad to have an intelligent, brilliant mind, as long as that mind is submissive to the leading of the Holy Spirit. The apostle Paul was a brilliant man, yet he learned to trust the illumination of the Holy Spirit rather than the carnal mind. God used Paul's educational training for His glory, but Paul did not rely on it.

I am supportive of intellectual pursuits and education. I want young people to attend universities and finish their studies. I have helped many of them to reach their goals and graduate. The problem with intellectualism arises when we try to use our carnal minds to understand something spiritual or to activate the supernatural power of God. Then, our minds become the enemy because they try to replace divine revelation. If we surrender to the carnal mind, we end up doubting God's power.

I consider myself to be an intelligent person. I am an avid student who loves to learn. By God's grace, I have earned several degrees. However, at the outset of my ministry, I had a difficult time trying to understand God with my mind until I recognized that He could be understood only through revelation by the Holy Spirit. It was then that I totally surrendered my mind to the Lord so that He could fill it with His thoughts. This is the reason why the apostle Paul urged us to *"be transformed by the renewing of your mind"* (Romans 12:2).

What Happened at the Beginning of Creation?

The fall of man occurred when Adam substituted mental knowledge and common sense for the revelation of God. He disobeyed the command of God:

> But of the tree of the knowledge of good and evil you shall not eat. (Genesis 2:17)

After Adam sinned, time, space, and matter became the foundation of his reality. Sin took from him the ability to see into the spiritual realm. This is the reason the carnal mind has problems dealing with anything it cannot explain and has trouble understanding God and His supernatural power. Today, the carnal mind still determines our reality until we are born again. When we receive Jesus, we begin the process of renewing our minds with God's thoughts. What God has done, is doing, and will do in the future is beyond our understanding. Our reality is determined by the level of revelation we have from Him. Our intellect causes us to tend to continue in the natural dimension, thereby creating limitations in our lives, unless we tap into God's supernatural knowledge.

But God did not leave us as slaves to our intellect. After the fall, He gave us faith to enable us to exit the natural realm in which we had fallen. Faith is the "antenna" by which we can see into the spiritual realm; it then allows us to take action in the physical realm. If God's intention was for mankind to remain only in the natural realm forever, He never would have given us faith.

What Can Take Us beyond the Natural (or Worldly) Dimension?

- Revelation, or revealed knowledge
- Faith

By nature, the carnal mind is anti-God.

So then, those who are in the flesh cannot please God.
(Romans 8:8)

Common sense, logic, and reason cannot produce miracles. They cannot make a blind man see or a deaf-mute hear or speak. They cannot cure cancer or make cysts disappear. We need to raise a generation of believers who are not afraid or skeptical of the supernatural.

While I was rebuking demons during a crusade in Barranquilla, Colombia, a child was brought to me. His arm was soon to be amputated due to gangrene, which had set in after an accident. When I prayed for him, the power of God descended upon that child, and he was healed. Immediately, he was able to move the arm that had been paralyzed. At the end of my trip, I asked my son, Ronald, what moment of the crusade had made the greatest impact on him. He said that he would never forget the miracle God had given that child. My son is well rooted in the supernatural because he has seen, heard, and personally experienced God's power from a young age.

Common sense and human reasoning can never produce a miracle.

Today's generation does not know that it can go beyond medical diagnoses, beyond financial problems, and beyond all natural evidence. This is why believers must announce the Good News and tell people that Jesus lives and that He is powerful to do far more than what the human mind can fathom.

In another crusade, a man who was visiting the church for the first time went home with a powerful miracle. For eight months, he had been connected to an oxygen tank 24/7 because he was suffering from pulmonary fibrosis, a serious disease that causes progressive scarring of the lung tissue, making breathing difficult and painful. On that day, I was preaching about our supernatural God—our heavenly Father—and I presented to the church a Jesus who is full of power to perform miracles. This man's faith was activated by what he heard, and he came to the altar in front of the entire congregation. He took off the oxygen mask and was able to breathe with ease. The Lord had healed him instantly!

The Church of Human Ability

The church today tends to operate on the basis of human abilities. If something doesn't fall within the scope of what is considered "normal," it is not to be believed. Consequently, nothing supernatural ever happens. The result is that people attend church without expecting to see anything extraordinary or supernatural take place. Why, then, do we even go to church? Would we go to our jobs if we didn't expect to be paid? Would we go to a restaurant if we didn't expect to eat? Why would we go to church if we don't expect to witness miracles or experience some supernatural event—a healing, a new song, a new sign, or a miracle? If none of these occurs in the church, something is not right.

Why does the church not expect anything supernatural to take place? Because it doesn't know how to bring the supernatural into the services. It lacks a revelation of the supernatural, eternal, and all-powerful God. Humanism has robbed us of this expectancy. Many leaders and ministers have become stagnant and irrelevant, failing to generate any change or effect an impact within their nations or churches. The time has come to retake the path set by the early church and return once again to the revelation of the living Christ, raised, all-powerful, and supernatural.

Summary

- God is a spiritual being with supernatural abilities. He lives in eternity but manifests His presence in our physical dimension.

- Revelation is the revealed knowledge of God that comes directly into our spirits in an instant, without prior knowledge or research.

- The Holy Spirit is the only Source of revelation we need to know God.

- All the mysteries of wisdom are hidden in Jesus and are available to the humble who hunger to know God intimately.

- The four things that can be known only through revelation are God's nature, human nature, the origin of man, and the origin of life.

- The two sources of supernatural power are God and Satan.

- God created man with an instinctual desire for power.

- The five enemies of supernatural power are ignorance, bad theology, humanism, the spirit of Jezebel, and the carnal mind.

- Faith and revelation enable us to live beyond the natural dimension.

Action Steps

- If you genuinely desire to know the supernatural God, ask the Holy Spirit to open your understanding and reveal His greatness, His majesty, His love, and His supernatural power.

- Receive this prayer: Right now, I declare by faith that your eyes, ears, and spiritual senses will be opened to receive a supernatural experience with the living, real, supernatural Christ.

2

Substitutes for the Supernatural Power of God

I would like to share part of my testimony with you because I believe it is important to know what God can do in anyone who makes himself available to Him.

I was born in Honduras, Central America, in 1965. I came to the United States at a young age, and I have lived here more than half my life. At the age of twenty-one, I accepted Jesus as my Lord and Savior at the Catedral del Pueblo Church in Miami, Florida—the largest Hispanic church in the country at that time. In 1988, God called me to preach His Word, so I enrolled at the Living Word Biblical Institute. After graduation, I spent the next nine years preaching the gospel in more than forty countries. Finally, in 1996, I founded King Jesus Church in Miami with a congregation of only twelve people. Today, we have over fifteen thousand active members, with another four thousand members at our "daughter churches."

In 2000, God called me into an apostolic ministry in which several renowned apostles and prophets within the body of Christ have confirmed my calling and established me as an apostle. I founded the New Wine Apostolic Network, which offers spiritual covering to more than one hundred churches and pastors in twenty-five countries. The vision of the network is to evangelize, affirm, disciple, and send. Furthermore, I also host a radio and television program, *Time for Change*, which is heard and seen through an extensive network of radio and television stations around the world.

My Mission on Earth

While praying and seeking God's presence, I experienced a supernatural visitation in which He spoke to my heart, saying, *I have called you to bring My supernatural power to this generation.* In the midst of my tears and trembling, I heard the same voice once more, only this time, it was audible and seemed to be right there in the room with me. It said, "I have called you to bring My supernatural power to this generation." Two weeks later, a prophet and friend, Hank Kunneman, called to tell me that the Holy Spirit had revealed to him that it was God who had visited me. He gave me a Bible verse as confirmation of the voice's message:

> *For this very purpose I have raised you up, that I may show My power in you, and that My name may be declared in all the earth.* (Romans 9:17)

Since that day, my mission has been to bring the supernatural power of God to this generation by teaching, training, and equipping church leaders and believers to manifest that power on earth. In line with my mission, this book is for those who deeply desire to experience God's supernatural power so that they may bless a world that now stands in crisis and hopelessness. To understand and operate in that power, I believe we need revelation and understanding of the kingdom of God.

What Is the Kingdom of God?

The kingdom of God is the invisible, divine government that is established on earth when the will of its King has been carried out completely. It is His administration influencing the earth, replacing its mundane operating system and order. The kingdom of God is the lordship and dominion on earth of King Jesus manifested in a visible form.

SUBSTITUTES FOR THE SUPERNATURAL POWER OF GOD ⌐ 41

Jesus spoke of three divine realms:

*For Yours is the **kingdom** and the **power** and the **glory** forever.* (Matthew 6:13, emphasis added)

The *"kingdom"* is the government of God; the *"power"* is the ability found in God; the *"glory"* is the presence of God.

The essence of Jesus' teaching is the kingdom, the power, and the glory.

In Acts 1, Jesus spent around forty days teaching His disciples about the kingdom. His goal was to prepare them for the day when they would receive the power, an event that takes place in chapter 2 and is followed in chapter 3 by the manifestation of God's glory. Today, some ministries teach much about God's kingdom but with little demonstration of His power. In other ministries, the opposite occurs—there is a great manifestation of God's power, but little mention is made of the kingdom. In still other ministries, there is teaching on the glory but no manifestation of the power or God's kingdom. Jesus taught His disciples about the kingdom because He understood that to be effective witnesses in a hostile world, they would need the power. Furthermore, He knew that the government and the religious leaders of the day would do anything to eliminate any evidence left behind that might prove His resurrection.

What Generates the Revelation of the Kingdom in the Believers?

• **Structure**

The revelation of the kingdom produces within our spirits a knowledge of how to use God's authority and how to submit to it. Without this knowledge, such power may destroy people. The subjugation of Satan can be understood only by revelation from the kingdom of God. When we finally understand this, we will see the undeniable superiority of the kingdom of light each time it confronts the kingdom of darkness.

- **Order**

Order cannot be established in the absence of government and authority. Without them, chaos and disorder can become dangerous when faced with the power of God.

- **Vision**

In the absence of vision, principles, character, and a kingdom mentality, supernatural power could be used for other things and not for the expansion of God's kingdom and the blessings He has for His people. Without the kingdom's vision, power can become futile or destructive.

- **Purpose**

Knowledge—or revelation—of the kingdom must come first in our lives. That principle is still active today. We live in a society that is hostile toward the gospel. It is full of wickedness and iniquity, and, without His power, we would never be able to succeed in it.

What Is the Power of God?

The Greek word for "power" is *dynamis*. This word also means "powerful force, potency, or inherent power." *Dynamis* is the ability to perform miracles. It is the explosive, dynamic, and inherent power of God—His supernatural ability. Many Christian circles exhibit a negative attitude toward this power because they have never personally experienced or witnessed a physical miracle or a supernatural occurrence. His power is intrinsically tied to the message of the gospel, and this is the difference between Christianity and other religions that cannot produce a supernatural experience. In the book of Acts, the supernatural power of God is present in each of its twenty-eight chapters. At present, countless churches are full of people who are sick and oppressed because they have replaced the power with other things.

> ## Religion is the result of not having an experience with God.

The church that Jesus left behind in the first century evangelized and established the kingdom using supernatural power as their primary tool. However, with the passing of time—and the influence of the spirit of witchcraft—the expectation of God's supernatural power has been abandoned, producing the need to seek idealized human tricks and talents as substitutes for the miraculous.

Substitutes for the Power of God

> ## The spirit of witchcraft is in operation wherever you find carnal habits and legalistic practices.

Therefore He who supplies the Spirit to you and works miracles among you, does He do it by the works of the law, or by the hearing of faith? (Galatians 3:5)

The Galatians had started out in the Spirit: they were saved, were filled with the Spirit, and witnessed miracles, signs, and wonders. But witchcraft influenced them to follow unbiblical rules, norms, and carnal ways, which caused them to lose sight of God's power.

The church today is in a similar situation. Most Christian movements, regardless of denomination, began with a supernatural revelation from God. Without this, they never would have been able to make an impact in the world. But, how many of them are still operating under the supernatural power with which they began? Sadly, very few. At some point, the human soul became a substitute for the Holy Spirit.

Let us recall that man is a spirit who has a soul and lives in a body. The soul has legitimate functions, but it cannot take the place of the spirit. When people begin to put their trust in their own abilities and strength, they move away from the spirit and toward the soul, which includes intellect and emotions. Then, a substitution takes place in which "religion" takes over for spiritual reality. Let us look at some of the most common substitutes.

- **Theology, lacking inspiration from the Holy Spirit, replaces revelation.**

Theology is man studying God with his human mind and reasoning. This is a proper way to study Him, but in order for it to be effective, man needs the revelation of the Holy Spirit. In other words, mankind needs to balance the knowledge he derives from studying God's Word with the knowledge he gets from the Holy Spirit. This combination of the Spirit and the Word is what transforms our lives.

- **Intellectual education replaces character.**

Education occupies an important place in the life of an individual. Thus, it is important for young people to study, pursue educational degrees, and become excellent professionals. However, we must keep in mind that intellectual education does not build or shape their character; it only prepares them to carry out a job. The only thing that can shape character and transform the heart of man is the power of God.

It is very dangerous to train people intellectually without dealing with their character.

When the carnal (worldly) mind is educated without character training, a well-educated enemy of God results. Some theological seminaries do not believe in the supernatural revelation of the Holy Spirit. Because their only goal is to educate minds without shaping character, their students become enemies of the gospel of the kingdom.

- **Psychology and psychiatry replace spiritual discernment.**

Psychology is part of the philosophy that studies the soul and the mind. Psychiatry is the science that studies the psyche of the human mind and the illnesses connected to it. God gave us perception and discernment, both of which help us to discover the root causes of our problems. However, instead of using these, we sometimes seek answers to our spiritual problems with psychological and psychiatric strategies and methods. Psychologists and psychiatrists have the best intensions to help people, but they do not deal with the roots of their problems, which are spiritual. They deal only with the symptoms—the branches, which are superficial.

- **Man-made programs replace the leading of the Holy Spirit.**

The Bible teaches that in order for our works to prosper, God must take the initiative. (See, for example, Proverbs 16:3; 16:9 NIV.) Unfortunately, many churches carry out their services according to their own agendas. Some even plan activities two or three years in advance without allowing any room for whatever the Holy Spirit might want to do. This is one reason we see such powerlessness within the church.

- **Eloquence replaces the demonstration of power.**

Many preachers fail to impart transformation to the hearts of people because they leave out the most important ingredient: the power of God. People run after personality-driven churches that are built on human charisma, talents, and gifts instead of on the name of Jesus.

- **Administrators replace apostles and prophets.**

Apostles and prophets bring the revelation and power that create breakthrough within the church. They are empowered by God with the anointing for spiritual warfare. When we substitute administrators for apostles and prophets, we essentially take much of God's power away from the church.

- **Reason, logic, and a carnal mind replace living by faith.**

When we handle divine situations with a carnal mind, we limit God and lose hold of the supernatural. Faith gives us the ability to believe above human reason because it supersedes all reasoning. Many of the things the Lord did in the Bible did not make sense to those who witnessed them.

- **Motivational preaching replaces the message of the cross.**

Motivational preaching is good because it inspires people, but when it is done without Jesus Christ as its central figure, it has no power to change hearts. To eliminate or hide Jesus within a message so as not to offend is the same as nullifying the power He activated with His death and resurrection.

- **Rigid laws, norms, and regulations replace love.**

Many churches are more concerned with people keeping the traditions, norms, rules, and regulations of the council or denomination than offering the genuine love of Christ to the lost. Love is the only thing that can loosen God's power.

- **Entertainment replaces power.**

Many believers attend church in search of entertainment, and many leaders use entertainment as a means of keeping membership numbers high without fully establishing anyone in the power of God. This is another reason why so many of God's people do not experience the supernatural in their lives.

When we entertain people, we have lost the power.

- **Human ability replaces God's grace.**

Grace is the divine ability given by God for His people to become everything He has called us to be and to achieve that which we are unable to do in our own strength. There are men and women of God who have a supernatural ministry, but their character fails to measure up. As a result, other people reject them and thereby reject the supernatural. This is when God's grace intervenes—when we are unable to achieve things in our own strength. Christ was the only perfect Man, and His life was a manifestation of God's supernatural power. He maintained a balance between His power and His character. If He was able to do it, then we should also be able to do it—with His grace, of course.

> *He who believes in Me, the works that I do he will do also; and greater works than these he will do, because I go to My Father.* (John 14:12)

- **Traditions replace the Word.**

> *You...[make] the word of God of no effect through your tradition which you have handed down.* (Mark 7:13)

In some Christian circles, it is common to hear preaching that is based on traditions that have been passed down from generation to generation. The leaders in these churches fail to realize that their method of preaching nullifies the effect of the Word of God. The fact that many of these churches are part of a long-standing tradition does not necessarily mean the tradition comes from God. In fact, if a tradition fails to produce new life or transform people's lives, it is probably not of God. Tradition is not a substitute for the Word and the Holy Spirit, which are the only things that can truly change lives.

Once we become aware of all the things that many churches substitute for the power of God, we begin to recognize why so many in the church lack power, as this is why miracles, healings, and salvations occur so rarely. If you are operating under any of the aforementioned substitutes, repent and return to God in order to manifest His supernatural power to this generation. The following prayer will help you achieve that:

My Lord Jesus, I repent of replacing Your power with human substitutions. I ask You to fill me once more with Your supernatural power, which I need to carry out Your purpose here on earth.

Ask the Lord to fill you with His power right now!

Balancing Supernatural Power

- ## Power and character

In many congregations, there is a negative attitude toward anything that borders on the supernatural, whether in the church or the world. Some people look at their flawed leaders and say, "I don't believe in miracles, in healing, or in the power of God because the man who performs such miracles has terrible character." Although character is not a requirement for obtaining a gift, it is important in pursuing holiness and honoring the Giver of the gift and His gospel. If we say, "You have the supernatural but lack character," we might say to someone else, "You have character, but where are the miracles?" Jesus, with His holy character, manifested miracles everywhere He went. However, in Scripture, we also find men who lacked character, had supernatural ability, and were greatly used by God. For instance, regardless of how he ended his life, Samson is still counted as one of the heroes of the faith. (See Judges 13–16.) Our character should be formed so that it is able to match the level of power we receive. Only then will we find balance and success. Therefore, it is important to have a mentor—a spiritual mother or father—who can equip and train you in God's supernatural power and also help you to shape and maintain your character.

On the other hand, if we give character more emphasis than power, we turn the gifts of the Holy Spirit into a reward. In other words, they are no longer gifts but rewards or blessings for good behavior. As a man committed to demonstrating the character and power of God, I cannot say that one is less important than the other, but it is a mistake to think that we can be more effective if we dedicate time and effort to shaping our character while setting aside the manifestation of power.

- ## Power and authority

As we've said, the Greek word *dynamis* means "strength, power, ability," while the Greek word *exousia* means "the power of authority (influence) and of right (privilege)...jurisdiction."

Behold, I give you the authority [exousia].... (Luke 10:19)

When a person has *dynamis* (power) but lacks *exousia* (authority), he may find himself in a grave situation because of this imbalance. The duration of supernatural power is directly proportional to the level of authority in which a person operates. If you do not honor authority, you might be able to perform miracles, signs, and wonders, but your lack of submission and surrender will begin to manifest in diminished results because the power will expose flaws in the flesh.

When I traveled as an evangelist, I met a pastor in another country who had a church with thousands of members. God was powerfully using him to perform miracles, signs, and wonders, but he did not submit to authority and refused all words of counsel. Eventually, at a time when his church was extremely effective, it was discovered that he was involved in an adulterous affair with a woman from his leadership team. In time, other sinful activities were also discovered in his life. Because of his sin, his ministry was eventually destroyed. Sadly, this is a clear example of what can happen when there is an imbalance of power and authority in your life.

Authority is the ability to exercise the power that leads to Godlike behavior.

- **Word and Spirit**

  For there are three that bear witness in heaven: the Father, the Word, and the Holy Spirit; and these three are one. (1 John 5:7)

When we preach and teach God's Word, we must always wait for the manifestation of the Holy Spirit. I devote time during each service to teach from God's Word and to minister what the Holy Spirit has for His people. This demonstrates the power of the preached Word. An imbalance occurs when people focus only on the Word and never allow the Holy Spirit to move freely, or when they focus only on manifestations of power and neglect the priority of the Word. But if we keep these two—the Word and the Spirit—in balance, we will experience the full blessings of God.

It is possible to have an experience and to be deceived, but not having an experience is already a deception.

- ## Power and harvest

We must understand the relationship between revival and harvest. I define *revival* as "receiving the power to go and gather the harvest of souls." If we fail to gather the harvest, our revival experience has been in vain. You are chosen, equipped, and anointed to go throughout the world in search of souls and to perform miracles, signs, and wonders. Many people stop for an "upper room experience" (see Acts 2:1–4) and never get around to gathering the harvest, even as people all around them remain ignorant of the gospel and bound for an eternity in hell. We can fill ourselves with power yet remain seated on our church pews, doing nothing. When this happens, we grow cold toward the things of God. But He has anointed us to gather the harvest and not to remain benchwarmers.

- ## Words and actions

Jesus of Nazareth...was a Prophet mighty in deed and word before God and all the people. (Luke 24:19)

The complete power of the kingdom can manifest only when words and actions are aligned.

Jesus operated in words and actions.

The former account I made, O Theophilus, of all that Jesus began both to do and teach.... (Acts 1:1)

God's Word always shows Jesus...

- Doing
- Teaching

Without faith, the kingdom will not have maximum impact.

Believe Me that I am in the Father and the Father in Me, or else believe Me for the sake of the works themselves.

(John 14:11)

Theology without works is a dead science.

The multitudes followed Jesus not because they wanted to join a church but to hear about His kingdom and to see the wonders and miracles He performed. After demonstrating the power, Jesus presented the kingdom. This concept appears over and over again throughout the Gospels.

This has also happened to me in countries where people are reluctant to accept the gospel. Often, the only way to soften their hearts is to demonstrate God's power. After praying for the sick, I demonstrate the power with a person who is missing a bone, has a cyst, or is blind or deaf—someone in desperate need of a physical healing miracle. After people witness the miracle, they are sensitized and ready for the calling of salvation. They are eager to answer the call, walk to the altar, and receive their salvation.

There are two things we should avoid in our relationship with the Holy Spirit if we want to achieve balance in our character: grieving the Holy Spirit and quenching Him.

- **Do not grieve the Holy Spirit.**

And do not grieve the Holy Spirit of God, by whom you were sealed for the day of redemption.

(Ephesians 4:30)

In Greek, the word for *"grieve"* is *lypeo*, which means "to make sorrowful, to affect with sadness, cause grief, to throw into sorrow...offend."

How do we grieve the Holy Spirit? We do so by having bad or evil attitudes, thoughts, or actions, and by having angry outbursts, slanderous conversations, and bitter quarrels. We also grieve the Holy Spirit when we deliberately participate in sinful activities. When we live in anger, wrath, and deception, we impede the Holy Spirit from flowing through us. Therefore, we grieve Him.

- **Do not quench the Holy Spirit.**

"Do not quench the Spirit" (1 Thessalonians 5:19). What does it mean to quench the Holy Spirit?

In Greek, the word for *"quench"* is *sbennymi*, meaning "to extinguish...of fire or things on fire...to suppress, stifle." It also implies the idea of obstructing the flow of something—to drown out, kill, or block the source. Jesus said, *"He who believes in Me...out of his heart will flow rivers of living water"* (John 7:38). He did not talk of drops of water or a trickle of water but *"rivers."* To quench the Holy Spirit is to cut off His flow and dry up the spring. It is like crimping a hose of running water to stop the flow. When we experience anger, bitterness, slander, and other sins in our lives, we are blocking the Holy Spirit from flowing through us. In doing so, we essentially quench His power.

At our church, the services occasionally take longer than expected. This happens because the Holy Spirit of God is moving—healing, delivering, and saving those who desperately need it. However, when I have been forced to cut services short for one reason or another, I immediately realize that I have quenched the flow of the Holy Spirit, which then stops the power of God from operating at that particular moment.

Jesus modeled how we should live with the Holy Spirit without grieving or quenching Him.

There was time when I did not understand why many pastors who love God and His people fail to experience the power of God in their lives or their churches. Although they may have not quenched the Spirit in their personal lives, I now realize that they did so in their ministries by denying the Holy Spirit the freedom to use them to prophesy, to move in His gifts, to pray for the sick, or even to dance under His control. Each time the Holy Spirit of God inspires them to do so, they suppress or stifle Him. Again, this is often the reason their churches lack power. I had to repent before God for the many times I quenched and suppressed the Holy Spirit of God when I denied Him the freedom to flow as He wills.

As Christians, we should daily strive not to grieve or quench the Spirit in order to maintain a good relationship with the Holy Spirit.

Grieving the Holy Spirit deals with our character; quenching the Holy Spirit deals with power.

Let me give you an example of this. On one occasion, an evangelist in our church was on his way to Florida International University when God gave him a vision of students wearing red shirts. As he entered the university's library, he saw a student wearing a red shirt leaving the premises. He immediately walked over to him and began to tell him about Jesus. In response, the young man kept repeating that he was an atheist. Then, he asked the evangelist how he was so certain which god was the true God since Allah, Buddha, and Jesus all easily fit the description of a god. The evangelist simply replied, "You have experienced moments of great risk in which you were in danger of losing your life, but you have not died, because of God's infinite mercy." The young man could not understand everything he was hearing, but he admitted that these words were true. "I have seen many people die in the Iraq war," he said, "but I have escaped death. I have often wondered why I was spared." At that moment, the power of God came upon him, and his legs began to shake. He asked the evangelist, "How did you know this?" The evangelist answered, "Well, you asked me how I know who the true God is, and now I say to you that the One who revealed this to me was not Allah or Buddha, but Jesus—the only true God!" The young man immediately said, "Now, I believe!" He instantly received Jesus as his only Lord and Savior.

A ministry that performs miracles but fails to gather the harvest of souls is not fulfilling the complete will of God.

Power without balance can destroy the user along with those around him. However, if power is used with wisdom and balance, it can impact thousands of lives in positive ways, glorify God, and, above all, result in a great harvest of souls.

Summary

- The revelation of the kingdom produces a structure—order, vision, and purpose—that prepares us to receive the power.

- Supernatural power is the explosive, dynamic, and intrinsic ability of God to do anything.

- The substitutes of power we must avoid are: uninspired theology; intellectual education; psychology and psychiatry; man-made programs; eloquence; administrators; reason, logic, and a carnal mind; motivational preaching; rigid laws, norms, and regulations; entertainment; human ability; and traditions.

- Power is balanced by character, authority, the Word and the Spirit, the harvest, and words combined with actions.

3

The Purpose of God's Supernatural Power

For twenty-two years, a man had been controlled by a spirit of alcoholism. It was a generational curse that had been rooted within his family's bloodline for three generations. Then, one day, this man saw me on television. He watched as I called over the airwaves for viewers to throw away their liquor. At that moment, he felt such a conviction in his spirit that he obeyed by throwing out his supply of beer. Immediately, he was fully convinced that it was God who was speaking to him. Since that day, he has served the Lord wholeheartedly, never again touching a drop of alcohol. Today, he is a mentor whose testimony edifies other people who are facing the same problem. Thanks to our loving Lord, that generational curse was broken in this man and in his family. And it all happened when God used a television program to do His will.

Everything created by God has a specific purpose. God never creates anything at random. If He gave us His supernatural power through His Son, Jesus, it is because we need it to carry out the Great Commission He gave us. When we ignore the purpose of something, we pervert its function, people use it ineffectively, and negative results ensue. In this chapter, we will discover the purpose of God's supernatural power and how to receive and handle it properly.

55

The Main Objectives of God's Supernatural Power

Jesus did not give us His power in vain. He had clear, specific objectives in mind that are directly related to the advancement of His kingdom on earth. Let us look at eight of those objectives:

1. The formation and edification of Christian character

Character cannot be changed on the basis of personal ideas, concepts, philosophies, achievements, rules, norms, or disciplines. To effect change in character, we need God's supernatural power. Religion—following laws to please God—cannot change man's inner self; this can happen only by God's supernatural grace. I define *grace* as "the undeserved gift of God's supernatural power that helps us to do what we cannot do on our own and to be what we cannot be by our own strength or merits."

Grace is God's divine power that helps us to obey God and function like Him.

2. The development of an effective prayer life

Jesus said, *"The spirit indeed is willing, but the flesh is weak"* (Matthew 26:41). Therefore, if you want to develop a life of continuous prayer through discipline, commitment, and perseverance, it can be accomplished only if you also add the fundamental ingredient of God's power. Then, when your flesh refuses to seek God, you need to ask for His grace to withstand all temptation, and you do this by faith.

3. The fulfillment of ministerial functions and service to God

Serving God effectively is impossible if we depend on our own strength to do it. The preaching and teaching of the gospel must be anointed with supernatural power from God. Pastors may speak the words found in the Bible with great eloquence, but if the element of power is missing, they will not produce the desired effect. People who serve God without His power will eventually suffer from spiritual or emotional burnout.

4. Victory over sin

We cannot overcome sin in our own strength. When we deal with impure thoughts, bondage, and addictions on a daily basis by trying to overcome them with rigorous disciplines or powerless spiritual exercises, we can end up being destroyed by wickedness. Sin was conquered on the cross of Calvary. There, we received the power to live a clean, pure life. Consequently, sin no longer has a hold on us; rather, we have dominion and control over sin through the transference of power that Jesus provided at the cross.

5. The defeat of Satan and his demons

Everyone needs God's supernatural power to defeat Satan and his demons because we are in a continuous spiritual war against him. Many people fail to realize that the spirit realm is real, and that there are two kingdoms in conflict—the kingdom of God and the kingdom of darkness—and that we are in the middle of this war. Jesus defeated Satan at the cross, but believers have to take action and manifest that victory on earth.

6. An obedient heart

> *For I will not dare to speak of any of those things which Christ has not accomplished through me, in word and deed.* (Romans 15:18)

Teaching the Word of God without a demonstration of miracles will neither excite people nor enable radical changes in their lives. However, when miracles, signs, and wonders are evident, people will experience change almost immediately. Sometimes, we try to reach out to people through counseling, discipline, or pastoral care. These practices can be helpful, and they have their place within the ministry. I also practice them, but when miracles take place, they appeal to the spirit.

We can appeal to people's reason, but this will work for only a short time. The supernatural power of God alone can leave a permanent imprint on their spirit.

7. The ability to achieve great results in a short time

So when they had appointed elders in every church, and prayed with fasting, they commended them to the Lord in whom they had believed. (Acts 14:23)

I estimate that the apostles accomplished this feat in approximately six months. Some ministries take three to five years to equip elders, ministers, and pastors. Was something happening in the first-century church that we rarely see in the church today? Yes! The power of God was being manifested for all to see. When God's power manifests, it produces an atmosphere in which the Holy Spirit is able to transform and deliver those who have been in churches for a long time without ever experiencing real change.

One of my editors experienced this. She came from another country, where she had grown up in the Christian faith. When she came to our ministry, however, everything seemed so new that she had the sensation of knowing nothing. She asked herself, *Where was I all those years?* At the time, we were holding three services each Sunday and one each Thursday. I remember seeing her at many services, receiving the revelation and impartation of the Word. She had never experienced God's power in such a way as this. In one year, she matured and grew beyond what she had learned in her twenty-five years as a Christian. She'd had a hard time testifying about Jesus because she'd had no idea how to respond to questions posed by unbelievers. Today, she is a fearless witness because she acquired the revealed knowledge, and God's power supports her testimony. When she speaks, people are transformed. Now, she serves in the kingdom and makes a difference in the lives of those who know her.

A message full of God's power can make us advance in minutes to a place that would have taken years to reach in the natural.

8. Becoming effective witnesses for Christ

But you shall receive power when the Holy Spirit has come upon you; and you shall be witnesses to Me in Jerusalem, and in all Judea and Samaria, and to the end of the earth. (Acts 1:8)

The most important objective for which God anointed us with His power is to become witnesses of Jesus' supernatural power. A witness is someone who personally experiences or acquires knowledge directly from the source and is capable of presenting evidence to prove what he or she saw or heard. The human mind is incapable of producing supernatural evidence; only God's power can do it.

We were created in God's image to do what He does.

God created us in His image. We are His representatives on earth, doing the same things He does. To do anything less would be an insult to Him. When do we receive the power to do what He does? We receive it when we are baptized—or filled—with the Holy Spirit. Jesus said,

But you shall receive power when the Holy Spirit has come upon you; and you shall be witnesses to Me in Jerusalem, and in all Judea and Samaria, and to the end of the earth. (Acts 1:8)

To this point, we could conclude that the main objectives for receiving God's supernatural power are: to shape our character, to establish an authentic prayer life, to serve God, to overcome sin, to defeat Satan, to develop obedience, to accomplish more in less time, and to become an effective witness for Jesus. Yet knowing these objectives is not enough. We must make the personal decision to commit ourselves and put His power into action. If we make this decision, God will support us and give us His power and grace to walk victoriously.

Conditions that Must Be Met to Be Filled with the Holy Spirit

According to God's Word, there are three conditions that must be met for us to be filled with the Holy Spirit and to operate in His supernatural power:

Behold, I send the Promise of My Father upon you; but **tarry** *in the city of Jerusalem until you are* **endued** *with* **power** *from on high.* (Luke 24:49, emphasis added)

The three conditions have corresponding words to identify them:

- Tarry
- Endued
- Power

In this verse, Jesus included these three words, giving His disciples the revelation to go in His name and manifest God's power to every creature as they carried out their ministry on earth. This same mission must be carried out today by each believer. Let us analyze each of those three words in detail.

Tarry

The Greek word for *"tarry"* is *kathizo*, which means "to make to sit down...to settle down." To tarry is to do more than merely wait or sit around doing nothing. The meaning of this word is intimately connected to a degree of authority, for another part of its meaning is "to set, appoint, to confer a kingdom on one."

But God...raised us up together, and made us sit together in the heavenly places in Christ Jesus.

(Ephesians 2:4, 6)

Thus, we are to remain comfortably seated on the throne—our seat of authority through Christ—with a sense of belonging and ownership and with the purpose of exercising authority to reign and to govern. In just a few words, Jesus told His disciples not to leave but to tarry—to remain until they learned how to sit comfortably on a throne, from which they would govern. Then, He gave them the power and the authority to govern.

I have identified three reasons why Jesus calls us to sit on a throne: (1) to govern in the political arena with authority; (2) to govern in the judicial and legal arena; and (3) to govern in the spiritual realm.

The phrase "to sit on the throne" should be applied in the same manner as it is used where we learn that Jesus is seated at the right hand of the Father. (See, for example, Colossians 3:1; Mark 16:19; Luke 20:42; and Psalm 110:1.)

God...made us sit together in the heavenly places in Christ Jesus. (Ephesians 2:4, 6)

Jesus taught from God's throne and spoke the Father's words. This is why He taught with such authority. We need to learn to do the same. From this day forward, every time we speak, teach, or preach, we must do so from the throne of authority. This is how we will obtain God's support. The reason Jesus was resurrected was to ascend to heaven and sit on the throne. From there, He sent us His Holy Spirit. Now, it is our turn, as the body of Christ, to sit on the throne and exercise the same authority.

Endued

The Greek word for "endued" is *endyo*, meaning "to sink into (clothing), put on." This refers to the way in which one might dye cloth. It is to be completely covered by a substance that cannot be removed so that it becomes inseparably ours. It is the idea of wearing something until it becomes "a second skin," indissoluble. This is what the anointing of the Holy Spirit does. If we are endued with the resurrected Christ, we become as one with Him. And He gives us the right color according to our personality.

> But **put on** *the Lord Jesus Christ, and make no provision for the flesh, to fulfill its lusts.*
> (Romans 13:14, emphasis added)

> **Put on** *the whole armor of God, that you may be able to stand against the wiles of the devil.*
> (Ephesians 6:11, emphasis added)

Are you clothed with *"the whole armor of God"*?

> *You have put off the old man with his deeds, and have* **put on** *the new man who is renewed in knowledge according to the image of Him who created him.*
> (Colossians 3:9–10, emphasis added)

Have you put on *"the new man"*?

These ideas are derived from the word *endued*—being completely submerged until you are inseparable from the element in which you are submerged.

This is not like putting on ceremonial attire that is worn for a time and then removed. Students who graduate from high school or college usually wear gowns and throw their caps into the air when the ceremony is over. Afterward, that cap and gown are never worn again. This is representative of the uncommitted Sunday believer who puts on the attire of king and priest and receives the anointing of the Holy Spirit but is incapable of rebuking a little cold after he or she walks away from the church. No! This is permanent attire. A committed believer will be clothed—endued—with the power of God.

Power

In Greek, we find several words that are used for various expressions of "power": *dynamai, dynamis, dynamoo, dunastes, dunateo, dynatos.* Let us look at three of their meanings.

• **Powerful (dynamoo)**

The word *dynamoo* is frequently used to describe everything God can do. In the New Testament, however, it is also used to describe what *we* who believe in Him can do. In other words, the Bible places God and His people in the same category—but only after we have been endued by the Holy Spirit with His power. Do not misunderstand me. I am not saying that we are gods or equal to God, but that we can do the same things God does when He imparts His power and His grace to us.

This word denotes the strong ability to do something or to carry out a task. It is to be physically and mentally able to do it, having the natural and logical abilities to do it.

Philippians 4:13 says, *"I can do [ischyo] all things through Christ who strengthens [endynamoo] me."* There are two words used here that relate to *power. Ischyo* means "to have power as shown by extraordinary deeds." If we were to do a literal translation of this verse, it might read, "I am powerfully equipped to do extraordinary deeds through Christ who empowers me."

Is there something specific in your life that you feel you should be able to do but can't do? If that is the case, through the revelation that comes from the Spirit, God assures you that you have the power to do it, in Him.

• **Able (dynamai)**

This word is used one hundred sixty-seven times in the *New King James Version.* It means "to be able to do something, to be capable, strong and powerful." It describes a person marked by intelligence, knowledge, and ability, one who is highly competent. God is able—*dynamai.*

Now to Him Who, by (in consequence of) the [action of His] power [dynamis] that is at work within us, is able [dynamai] to [carry out His purpose and] do superabundantly, far over and above all that we [dare] ask or think [infinitely beyond our highest prayers, desires, thoughts, hopes, or dreams]. (Ephesians 3:20 AMP)

- **Possible (*dynatos*)**

We find this Greek word fifteen times throughout the Bible. It means "able, powerful, mighty, strong...having power for something." It expresses the potential of something happening according to nature, tradition, or custom; something feasible that can come to pass.

Jesus looked at them and said to them, "With men this is impossible, but with God all things are possible."
(Matthew 19:26)

All things are *dynatos* for those who believe.

Jesus said to him, "If you can believe, all things are possible to him who believes." (Mark 9:23)

The word *power*, in all its various forms, appears in Scripture hundreds of times with a connotation of explosive power and ability.

- *Power*, as in ability, occurs ninety-five times having to do with God and ninety-five times having to do with the believer.

- *Power*, as in capability, occurs seventy-eight times relating to God being able and seventy-eight times relating to the believer being able.

- *Power*, as in possibility, occurs fifteen times referring to something that is possible for God and fifteen times referring to something that is possible for us.

- *Strengthened* appears sixteen times declaring we are as strong as God, with His strength.

- *Powerfully strong* appears twice declaring that God is powerful and twice declaring how powerful we are in Him.

In the New Testament, we find a large group of Greek words all deriving from the same root word, presented in different contexts, but all—for the most part—translated as *power, dominion, strength, ability,* and *energy.*

Jesus told His disciples—and tells us—to tarry so that the power of God could become one with theirs, a second skin that would make them inseparable from Him. Tomorrow, on your way to work or school or wherever you may go, wear your new royal attire. Assume the attitude and declare the Word, and then, when the enemy tries to attack your health or finances, remember that you have the power of heaven at your disposal.

God's power is evident in the following testimony: At the end of a church service, while I was greeting a group of people, a lady approached me and said that her doctor had diagnosed her esophagus as being nearly destroyed. He had insisted that she urgently needed an operation in order to restore it. At that moment, I embraced her, told her that God loved her, and said a short prayer—nothing fancy. When she returned to the doctor for preoperative tests, he was astonished to discover that her esophagus was completely healthy. No trace of her previous condition remained. Further testing confirmed that she had been completely healed. Since there was no need to operate, she was discharged from the hospital.

God had given this woman the creative miracle of a new esophagus. I did not heal her. God's power did as it was transferred to her body by means of a simple act of love: an embrace and a prayer. That was all it took for her to receive healing. Every disciple in my ministry is trained and equipped to walk under the same anointing that I have. Undoubtedly, a price must be paid—the price of sacrifice, holiness, obedience, love for your neighbor, and total surrender to God—in order for that anointing to be active in you. God wants to do the same things through you. Are you willing?

In the Bible, Jesus Sent His Disciples in Power

As you go, preach, saying, "The kingdom of heaven is at hand." Heal the sick, cleanse the lepers, raise the dead, cast out demons. Freely you have received, freely give.
(Matthew 10:7–8)

Today, Jesus Continues to Send Us— His Believers—in the Same Power

These signs will follow those who believe: in My name they will cast out demons; they will speak with new tongues.
(Mark 16:17)

God is God everywhere. I have preached in more than forty countries, and He has done the same things in all of them. He has never failed, not because I am special but because I make myself available. He wants to do it through you, too, if you will make yourself available to Him. He wants you to receive the revelation that you were created in His image and therefore can do the same things that He does. You need only to establish and maintain a close relationship with the Father and receive the infilling of the Holy Spirit. Then, go and preach the Good News everywhere. When you do this, God will confirm His Word.

My Personal Experience with God's Supernatural Power

The deaf and mute

During one service, when I started to walk down the aisle of the church, the Lord indicated to me that there was a person to my right whom He wanted to heal. I didn't know who it was, specifically. All I knew was that this person was deaf and mute.

When I called this person to come forth, someone helped a twenty-one-year-old Nicaraguan woman to come forward. She had been deaf and mute since birth. As soon as I prayed for her, her ears were opened, and her tongue was loosened. This miracle had a great impact because this young woman had never heard or spoken a word in her life. She had communicated only with sign language. What God did was so powerful that I asked her to give her testimony on our television program. A few days later, she returned, and her testimony was even more impressive because she had progressed in her speech. She was no longer speaking a word here and a word there; now, she was speaking fluidly. The community was deeply touched. This was the supernatural power of God!

Another day, during a Healing and Miracle Service, God urged me to pray for deaf-mutes, and I obeyed. Many were healed that day. Some began the process of hearing and speaking for the first time in their lives.

A twenty-eight-year-old African-American man was brought to the service. He had been deaf and mute since birth and was living, homeless, in one of the worst sections of Miami. It was beautiful to see the joy on his face as he smiled, looked surprised, and applauded with his hands. This young man received his miracle, and God was glorified in him. God poured out His love on this young life in such a way that the young man instantly received the ability to hear and speak. His healing was complete and absolute! He left leaping for joy, hearing and speaking of the wonders God had performed in his life. And the best part of this testimony is that the same miracles continue to take place everywhere I preach His Word. God wants to do miracles in your life, too!

The blind

During a Healing and Miracle Service in our church, the Spirit of God guided me to pray for the blind. Among the crowd was a twenty-two-year-old woman who had been born with a right eye that was completely blind. As the power of God descended upon the congregation and I declared the Word, she was touched by God and healed in a supernatural way. Instantly, her vision cleared. What doctors had been unable to do in twenty-two years, God did in an instant. When she realized that her sight had returned, she ran to the altar to give her testimony. The miracle was confirmed by the doctor who examined her. The Lord healed her to glorify His holy name and to demonstrate the fact that He continues to hear our prayers today and will forevermore. On that day, this woman walked away knowing that God had granted her the desire of her heart—vision in both of her eyes.

A paralytic

One man in our church was only twenty-five years old when a terrible automobile accident landed him in a hospital bed, where he heard the doctors give him a 4 percent chance of survival. The doctors also predicted that if he beat the odds and survived, there was an 87 percent chance that he would spend the rest of his life in a wheelchair.

At our church, we train people to pray and to know how to appropriate God's promises and loosen the power of the cross, especially when they face adverse circumstances. Taking what she had learned, this young man's mother began to pray at her son's bedside. With power, authority, and boldness, she claimed the promises of God for her son in the spirit realm. And the miracle took place! Against all odds, this young man held on to life, and, in only a few weeks, he began to show signs of improvement. Today, he lives and walks without difficulty. No traces of the accident are visible on any part of his body. His family and friends are still overwhelmed at the work of God's supernatural power in his life. During the healing process, the Lord began to prepare him for the time when he would impart to others what he had received through this experience. God never gives us something and expects us to remain stagnant. He always wants us to do something for others. This young man's mother had received the anointing for healing that I had imparted over her life, and she began to pray for her son. Today, God is ready to do the same for others.

The demon-possessed

During our Inner Healing and Deliverance Conference, I heard of a twenty-one-year-old woman who had multiple addictions that were controlling her life. She had tried everything humanly possible to overcome her addictions to marijuana and alcohol, but she had failed at each attempt. Furthermore, for years, she had dealt with extreme episodes of depression as a result of her brother's death. Consequently, her school grades were the worst she had ever produced. Her life was a major disaster until the day someone invited her to our church.

During her visit, I ministered deliverance and cast out every spirit of addiction to drugs and alcohol, loneliness, rejection, depression, grief, and mourning. I led her to forgive, to renounce her past, and to break away from all bondage. God delivered her from all of her afflictions and healed her soul. Jesus did the miracle! Today, her life is completely new. She is an honors student and a leader of a House of Peace, our all-church home fellowship ministry that also inspires young people to follow God. Our Lord is the only one who can deliver us from our afflictions and bring real change to our lives!

The dead

During one of our Healing and Miracle Services at a football stadium in Honduras, where over fifty thousand people had gathered, a pregnant woman came to the platform, accompanied by her doctor. The woman was crying inconsolably because the baby in her womb had been declared clinically dead a few days prior to the crusade. Because this woman's life would be in danger if the dead baby was allowed to remain in her womb, the doctor had ordered a dilation and curettage, a procedure that scrapes the uterine walls in order to remove the fetus. But this woman's faith was greater than the contradicting circumstances and the medical opinion concerning her condition. She had decided to take a personal risk and postponed the procedure so that she could attend the crusade and seek a miracle from God. Her doctor, concerned for his patient and not wanting to leave her alone, had decided to come along.

When I heard what this woman had done, I believed with her for a miracle and prayed for her. And God did it! Almost instantly, the baby began to move within her womb. A few minutes later, the astonished doctor testified that the baby was, indeed, alive. The mother testified, "God raised my baby from the dead. It is alive! It lives!" She repeated this over and over again. God's Word says that nothing is impossible for God. This was an incredible miracle. God raised a baby from the dead!

How to Operate in the Supernatural Power of God

1. Connect to Jesus, the only right Source of power.

Jesus said to him, "I am the way, the truth, and the life. No one comes to the Father except through Me."

(John 14:6)

Is there a "wrong" source of supernatural power? Many in this present generation are taking the wrong paths to find supernatural power: card readers, magic, masonry, the occult, yoga, witchcraft, astrology, horoscopes, tarot cards, telepathy, levitation, mental control, and New Age practices, such as metaphysics, parapsychology, and hypnotism. Some delve into acupuncture, astral projection, Santeria, or reincarnation. Others prefer to dabble in the false religious pursuits of Buddhism, Islam, Hinduism, Hare Krishna, and Rosicrucianism. Still others seek the supernatural through drugs, fame, wealth, prestige, or social status. All of these sources of power are "wrong," and those who practice them will eventually find their lives to be empty and desolate. Thus, it is imperative to connect to Jesus, the Son of God, who died on the cross, was raised from the dead, and now sits at the right hand of the Father with power, authority, and glory. Jesus is the only one who never changes. He lives. He's real. He is *"the same yesterday, today, and forever"* (Hebrews 13:8). He continues to perform miracles, signs, and wonders, as well as save the lost and transform mankind. Jesus is waiting for you to connect with Him.

2. Change your mind-set.

Do not be conformed to this world, but be transformed by the renewing of your mind, that you may prove what is that good and acceptable and perfect will of God.
(Romans 12:2)

It is essential to renew your mind so that you can have God's perspective and better bring the reality of heaven to earth. A mind that has not been renewed is unable to manifest the reality of that power on earth. When you renew your mind, you will be able to bring the reality of the supernatural world to earth and experience the will of God.

3. Learn to flow in power and compassion.

Compassion is heartache motivated by someone else's pain that prompts us to take action by doing something for the one who is suffering. Compassion was the principle that moved Jesus in His ministry.

Compassion without power is sympathy; power without compassion is professionalism.

The compassion that Jesus felt gave Him the anointing to receive the power, and it motivated Him to take action and accomplish His goal to destroy the works of the devil. Some have received His power before entering into His level of compassion. We must ask the Lord to give us the power and compassion to evangelize, heal the sick, and deliver the captives. The power is not for us but is intended to help us bless others.

Sympathy is a counterfeit version of compassion.

As you will learn through the following testimony, you and I were chosen and anointed with power to manifest God in this generation.

A minister and his youth group were driving through the city streets seeking souls to win for Christ, when, suddenly, God gave this minister a vision of a man wearing red shorts. While they were stopped at a convenience store, they spotted three African-American men, one of whom was wearing red shorts. They presented the gospel to them, and the Lord revealed to the minister that one of these men had knee problems and another suffered from asthma. Both men confirmed that this was true. Then, the minister said, "Before you confess Jesus as your Lord and Savior, He wants to show you His love and His power." As he said this, the minister placed one hand on the one man's bad knee and the other on the man with asthma and declared them healed. Immediately, the man with the bad knee began to shout that the pain in his knee was gone! His friend confirmed that he was now able to breathe again. He declared that he no longer felt the effects of his asthma. To confirm their healing, the minister invited them to run. The man with the bad knee took off in a sprint with no complaints of pain. The other man ran back and forth with no breathing problems whatsoever. God healed both men, and all three men received salvation. Praise the Lord!

Summary

- The objectives and areas in which we need God's power are character, prayer, ministry, and service. We also need His power to obtain victory over sin, to defeat Satan, to practice obedience, to obtain better results in less time, and to become effective witnesses for Jesus.

- The three conditions Jesus presented to His disciples and asks of us in order to move us into His supernatural power are summarized in the words *tarry, endued,* and *power.*

- In Scripture, three frequently used expressions of *power* are "powerful," "able," and "possible." Everything God does, we can do, and everything that is possible for God is also possible for the believer.

- In order to be able to do the things that God does, we need to have a relationship with Him and be filled with the Holy Spirit.

- The steps to moving in God's supernatural power are (1) connect to Jesus—the only right Source of supernatural power—in order to (2) have a change of mind-set and to (3) flow in His compassion.

4

Jesus and the Cross, the Only Legal Source of Supernatural Power

As I previously stated, this generation is looking for power in all the wrong places because it has not received the revelation of the cross. I consider it imperative for all people to receive that revelation because it redeems us from sin, defeats the devil, heals our sicknesses, and much more. How can we receive this gift of revelation? What happens when we preach the message of the cross? For most of mankind, the cross has become merely a piece of decorative jewelry that is worn around the neck or an ornate piece of lumber displayed in a church. The cross, however, symbolizes everything that Jesus did to carry out God's will on earth and to complete His redeeming work.

The death of Jesus can be divided into three parts:

- Physical torture and death on the cross
- Spiritual death
- Resurrection

Physical Torture and Death on the Cross

Jesus was crucified. Crucifixion is a form of capital punishment carried out by attaching a criminal to a tree. The custom probably started with the Medo-Persian Empire during the reign of the Macedonian king Alexander the Great, who is believed to have introduced the practice in Egypt and Carthage. It appears the Romans learned it from the Carthaginians, though it was the Romans who "perfected" this form of torture in a way that produced an agonizingly slow death with a maximum amount of physical and emotional suffering. It was truly one of the cruelest, most humiliating methods of execution, reserved specifically for slaves, murderers, traitors, and the vilest of criminals. Roman law protected its citizens from crucifixion, except for army deserters. For Israelites, a person who was crucified was seen as a curse.

> *If a man has committed a sin deserving of death, and he is put to death, and you hang him on a tree, his body shall not remain overnight on the tree, but you shall surely bury him that day,...for he who is hanged is accursed of God.*
> (Deuteronomy 21:22–23)

Specific Steps that Led to Jesus' Physical Death

- **He was whipped.**

> *Pilate, wanting to satisfy the crowd, released Barabbas to them; and he delivered Jesus, after he had scourged Him, to be crucified.* (Mark 15:15 NIV)

In Jesus' day, the whip was an instrument commonly used to inflict punishment. It was usually composed of several woven belts with small pieces of lead and sharp pieces of bone or sheep's teeth. To undergo the punishment, the criminal was undressed, tied to a pillar, and flogged. The lashes were directed toward the back, torso, and legs, and the severity of each lash depended on which part of the body it made contact with. The intent of the punisher was to weaken the victim to the point of passing out. Traditionally, this punishment was accompanied by verbal scorn and mockery. With each lash received, the lead pieces caused deep contusions, while the sharpened pieces of bone or teeth lacerated the skin and damaged the subcutaneous tissue. As the torture was applied, the cuts went deeper and deeper, causing increased damage to the muscle. The extreme pain and massive loss of blood often led to death due to circulatory shock.

- **His beard was plucked out.**

  I gave My back to those who struck Me, and My cheeks to those who plucked out the beard; I did not hide My face from shame and spitting. (Isaiah 50:6)

Plucking out the beard or hair was a major insult in Middle Eastern culture because the beard was a sign of virility and masculine dignity. This is the reason Jewish men grew and meticulously groomed their beards. God had ordained that men should not trim even the corners of their beards. (See Leviticus 19:27.) To shave or hide one's beard was a sign of humiliation, sadness, or mourning. So, when Jesus' beard was plucked out, it was not only extremely painful but also extremely humiliating.

- **His face was spat upon.**

  Then they spat in His face and beat Him; and others struck Him with the palms of their hands. (Matthew 26:67)

For Jews, spitting in the presence of others was an insult; spitting on someone was an even more grievous affront. When the Roman guards spit on Jesus' face, that was even worse.

- **He was forced to wear a crown of thorns.**

  And the soldiers twisted a crown of thorns and put it on His head. (John 19:2)

The crown of thorns was woven of thorn branches normally used to light fires. It is believed that the crown had more than three rows of thorns, and that it may have been shaped like a helmet, covering Jesus' head from the neck to the forehead.

Jesus' Health

Jesus' profession as a carpenter undoubtedly prepared Him for the rigorous demands of His ministry, which included walking across Palestine as He preached the gospel of the kingdom. It can be assumed that Jesus was in good health and did not suffer from either an illness or a weak constitution.

It is also reasonable to assume that Jesus was physically healthy as He faced His twelve-hour ordeal when, after a sleepless night, He was forced to walk approximately 2.5 miles coming and going through the streets of Jerusalem between the venues of His various trials. We must take into account the merciless punishment He received after the trial, the emotional stress of being abandoned by His closest disciples, the rejection He experienced at the hands of the people who had praised Him only a few days before, and, ultimately, His crucifixion.

Agony and Physical Death on the Cross

As was customary, the condemned man was made to carry his own cross from the place where he was whipped to the place outside of the city walls where he would be crucified. Historians maintain that the weight of these crosses was almost always over three hundred pounds. The gallows, or horizontal crosspiece, alone probably weighed between seventy-five and one hundred twenty-five pounds.

On the procession to the place of crucifixion, which was led by a centurion, the criminal was escorted by a Roman guard. One of the soldiers carried a sign on which was written the name of the criminal and the crime he had committed. Later, this would be placed on an upper portion of the cross for all to see. The Roman guard never left the offender until death was confirmed. After all the pain of the torture He had endured, Jesus' clothing was removed, and He was finally placed on the cross in an uncomfortable position that made breathing difficult. Added to this were dehydration caused by the loss of blood; fever, which only increased His thirst; the further humiliation of His naked suffering; and the scoffing and insults of a bloodthirsty crowd. If the Roman guard took pity on the victim, he might offer him a mixture of wine and myrrh, which served as a mild anesthetic. According to Scripture, Jesus refused this. (See Mark 15:23.)

At the moment of crucifixion, the criminal was thrown to the ground on his back. His arms were extended and were either nailed or tied to the gallows, the legs to the post. Apparently, Romans preferred nails to rope. Recently, archeologists discovered a crucified body dating back to the days of Jesus in a tomb close to the city of Jerusalem. They uncovered sharp iron nails approximately seven inches in length and one inch in diameter.

I am poured out like water, and all My bones are out of joint; My heart is like wax; it has melted within Me. My strength is dried up like a potsherd, and My tongue clings to My jaws; You have brought Me to the dust of death.
(Psalm 22:14–15)

Eventually, excess blood accumulated in the heart, blocking circulation, which, combined with the fever caused by trauma, tetanus, and exhaustion, often killed the victim in a matter of days or hours. In order to accelerate death, it was customary to break the offender's legs with a hammer, eliminating the ability of the victim to push up with the feet in order to breathe. On other occasions, the offender was pierced with a sword or spear or was asphyxiated with smoke.

[Jesus] *Himself bore our sins in His own body on the tree, that we, having died to sins, might live for righteousness; by whose stripes you were healed.* (1 Peter 2:24)

Jesus suffered all of that in our place. He allowed Himself to be treated as if He were the worst of criminals in order to redeem us from our sins. When we read the biblical account of this event, we realize the immense love God has for us—an unconditional love. Jesus died so that we could be free from sin and condemnation. If anyone doubts God's love, please, look to the cross and observe the exchange that was produced there out of love.

This was the physical death Jesus suffered. Now, let us consider His spiritual death.

Spiritual Death

Jesus' physical and spiritual deaths were both set into motion in the garden of Gethsemane. There, God the Father provided the Lamb that would redeem mankind from all its sins. Jesus was the Lamb without sin or blemish who offered His life for humanity. The Father essentially said to Him, "Son, You must carry the sins of the world; You will be the Lamb." No one can fathom how the Son of God—pure and holy and without sin—suddenly agreed to take upon Himself the filthy sins of the world. This is why, in the garden, He pleaded,

> *O My Father, if it is possible, let this cup pass from Me;*
> *nevertheless, not as I will, but as You will.*
>   (Matthew 26:39)

If you consider that the pain suffered by Jesus on the cross was horrible, His spiritual suffering was even greater, because He had to carry the concentrated and sickening filth of human sin—the iniquity and wickedness of mankind throughout time, ages, and generations. He bore all of the sins of resentment, homosexuality, hate, lies, rejection, generational curses, theft, abortion, murder, sexual abuse, sickness, idolatry, witchcraft, Satanism, and much more. He didn't just become sin, however; He also became the root of wickedness, or what the Bible refers to in Romans 7:18 as the *"sinful nature"* (NIV). It was in this condition that He climbed on the cross, and from there He shouted, *"My God, My God, why have You forsaken Me?"* (Matthew 27:46).

This was the first and final time that Father and Son would be separated by the barrier of man's iniquity. This was not a moment of communion for them, as martyrism was for Christian saints, who, as they were being stoned, burned, or devoured by lions, were often said to have been filled with God's peace and grace, which allowed them to die in peace. This is not what happened to Jesus. He was left completely alone, separated from the Father's presence and deprived of His grace. Because of our sin, God abandoned Jesus precisely when the Son needed His Father most. When we understand this, we can begin to love God more and to hate sin as He hates it.

So when Jesus had received the sour wine, He said, "It is finished!" (John 19:30)

In Greek, the word for *"finished"* is *teleo*, meaning "to bring to a close, to finish, to end…to perform, execute, complete, fulfill." Jesus said, in effect, "The debt has been satisfied completely; there is no more debt of sin." These words were not a cry of pain or anguish but of victory, like a gladiator after winning a death match. When we study the gospel accounts of Jesus' death, it is easy to perceive how cruel and horrible it was. Everything Jesus did at the cross, He did out of love for us. His physical and spiritual death loosened the supernatural power we needed to be forgiven, healed, and delivered.

The moment Jesus died, the veil in the temple ripped from top to bottom, signifying that the path to the Holy of Holies is now open. (See Matthew 27:50–51.) Then, the tombs of many of the dead saints were opened, and they began to walk throughout the city. (See verse 52.)

After Jesus surrendered His spirit and died, the centurion who stood guard at the foot of the cross marveled at the fact that Jesus was in total control of His execution, even to the point of choosing His moment of death. What he saw left him stunned, giving him no other choice but to kneel and recognize that Jesus truly was the Son of God. (See verse 54.)

Resurrection from the Dead

For as Jonah was three days and three nights in the belly of the great fish, so will the Son of Man be three days and three nights in the heart of the earth. (Matthew 12:40)

Sin and death had been conquered, but there were still things that needed to be done. As Jesus had prophesied above, He had to go to hell because that is what God's justice demanded. There, He took the keys of hell and death from Satan. The sting of death could not hold Him any longer. God the Father raised Him from the dead so He could sit on the throne of glory. God gave Him all power and authority over heaven and earth. Then, Jesus gave us the same power and authority to go in His name and proclaim the gospel of the kingdom throughout the world.

> *You shall receive power when the Holy Spirit has come upon you; and you shall be witnesses to Me in Jerusalem, and in all Judea and Samaria, and to the end of the earth.* (Acts 1:8)

The Revelation of the Cross

The cross is the sacrifice offered by Jesus for the human race, with all of its consequences and benefits. The cross implies two fundamental roles for the Son of God:

- **Jesus was the priest who offered the sacrifice.**

> *For such a High Priest was fitting for us...who does not need daily, as those high priests, to offer up sacrifices, first for His own sins and then for the people's, for this He did once for all when He offered up Himself.* (Hebrews 7:26–27)

- **Jesus was the sacrifice.**

> *For if the blood of bulls and goats and the ashes of a heifer, sprinkling the unclean, sanctifies for the purifying of the flesh, how much more shall the blood of Christ, who through the eternal Spirit offered Himself without spot to God...?* (Hebrews 9:13–14)

The word *"eternal"* means "without beginning and end, that which always has been and always will be." It surpasses the limits of time. The event at the cross changed history. It paid the wages of sin for all mankind, for all ages, for all centuries and millennia—past, present, and future, including the sins of those who have yet to be born.

The cross is the basis for God to provide absolute and total provision to mankind.

Everything we need, now and in the future—mentally, emotionally, materially, financially, or spiritually, be it power, authority, love, health, healing, or anything else—was provided at the cross. There is no other source. All the countless messages preached in churches and all the books on theological shelves are good, but none of them will work if we fail to appropriate the power of the cross.

The cross is the only genuine source of supernatural power.

It is time for the church to preach the message of the cross. The cross must be the central theme of every message. It must be given the highest priority. We cannot diminish the cross.

God told the nation of Israel to leave Egypt, and to raise an altar. They were not to place anything around it—not trees, decorations, or any objects that might separate the people from His presence. Let this be our example. We cannot surround the message of the cross with anything that robs it of power or diminishes the supremacy of Jesus. No religion in the world can equal the message of the cross.

The Cross: Abstract or Reality?

Philosophers speculate in the abstract, but the message of the cross is a real event in history and eternity. There is no

explanation other than it is real and true and the most important event in history. When we stop placing the cross at the
center of our message, our faith loses its meaning and we end
up in bondage to traditions, regulations, and laws that are
impossible to obey.

What Supernatural Power Did Jesus Loosen at the Cross?

*O foolish Galatians!...Are you so foolish? Having begun in
the Spirit, are you now being made perfect by the flesh?*
(Galatians 3:1, 3)

On the cross, Jesus loosened the supernatural grace of God.
Grace is an undeserved gift. It is His eternal presence—full of
power—that gives us the ability to be and to do everything we
cannot accomplish in our own strength. When we act without
God's grace, we become legalistic. This is what happened to the
Galatians. The same is happening to the church today. Hence,
there is an absence of power.

How does the enemy react to the work at the cross? Satan
counterattacks the work of Jesus at the cross with the spirit
of witchcraft. His goal is to darken the cross by provoking carnality, legalism, and paganism. This pattern has always been
evident in every congregation that has ever come under spiritual attack. Undoubtedly, legalism is the byproduct of carnality
produced by witchcraft.

What Is Legalism?

Legalism is the human effort to try to please God in our own
strength. It is an attempt to become holy or righteous through
rules, traditions, and laws. It adds other elements to the requi-
sites established by God that lead to righteousness. God asks
only that we believe, since we are justified by faith in Jesus and
in His redeeming work at the cross.

Christ has redeemed us from the curse of the law, having become a curse for us. (Galatians 3:13)

When a person trusts in his own strength to obtain salvation or to receive God's blessings, he automatically falls under the curse of the Galatians.

Legalism leads to witchcraft, and witchcraft leads to people falling under a curse.

The Two Great Works of the Cross

- **What the cross did *for* us**

Let us take a moment to consider the perfect work at the cross. The last words Jesus pronounced on the cross were, *"It is finished!"* (John 19:30). In effect, He said, "It is perfectly and completely done. It is done in eternity." When we understand the revelation of the complete and perfect work of the cross, we are then able to begin receiving all of its benefits.

- **What the cross did *in* us**

The work that was carried out by Jesus on the cross is rarely taught today. This lack of understanding causes many problems. You will never enjoy the benefits of the cross until you accept that it was designed to create a divine exchange. The essence of the cross consists in Jesus taking our place. He personally suffered the totality of the punishment that we deserved for our disobedience. In exchange, we received all the goodness that Jesus received for His obedience. Since that day, our goal should be to become like Jesus, just as He became like us.

The Divine Exchange

On the cross, God the Father placed all the consequences of the world's iniquity, guilt, shame, and rebellion on Jesus' shoulders. Understanding this revelation is key to receiving the benefits of the cross. A divine exchange was ordained at the cross, where every wicked thing produced by our rebellion was placed on Jesus, as all the goodness in Him became ours because of His obedience.

This exchange came about in the following way:

- **Jesus was wounded so we could be forgiven.**

  But He was wounded for our transgressions, He was bruised for our iniquities.   (Isaiah 53:5)

- **Jesus carried our sicknesses and suffered our sorrows so we could receive healing.**

  Surely He has borne our griefs (sicknesses, weaknesses, and distresses) and carried our sorrows and pains [of punishment], yet we [ignorantly] considered Him stricken, smitten, and afflicted by God [as if with leprosy]. But He was wounded for our transgressions, He was bruised for our guilt and iniquities; the chastisement [needful to obtain] peace and well-being for us was upon Him, and with the stripes [that wounded] Him we are healed and made whole.   (Isaiah 53:4–5 AMP)

Every time the Bible mentions the cross and the redeeming work that took place upon it, sickness is connected to it. However, it is always mentioned in the past tense indicating that healing already took place in eternity. Now, all we have to do is to appropriate the health that Jesus offers.

To better illustrate what I have just said, let us read what happened to a friend of mine, the director of a well-known Christian university:

In July 2009, at seventy-five years of age, a friend of mine was flying between Reno, Nevada, and San Antonio, Texas. At thirty thousand feet, he began to experience strong chest pains and to sweat profusely. At that moment, he could see the word *aspirin* in his mind. He asked the flight attendant to get him one, but she said that they did not carry medicine on board. The person sitting behind him, however, was a nurse, and she gave him an aspirin. A doctor seated a few rows back approached him and, with the nurse's help and a portable device she happened to be carrying, proceeded to give my friend first aid to keep him stable.

When the plane landed in San Antonio, my friend was taken to the hospital, where he went directly into surgery. When the doctors performed the preoperative checkup, they discovered that an operation was not needed due to the excellent medical attention he had received on the airplane. He had suffered a cardiac arrhythmia that could have killed him instantly had it not been for the opportune intervention of the doctor and nurse. My friend never saw the doctor or nurse again. He never got their names or contact information, but, as far as he is concerned, they were angels placed there by the Lord to keep him safe.

In October of the same year, this same friend found that he was unable to sleep due to his allergies. For fourteen days, he took two tablets of ibuprofen each day, hoping it would help him sleep. Unbeknownst to him, the frequent use of ibuprofen was causing stomach ulcers that went undetected because he was not suffering from pain or discomfort. When he noticed his skin color begin to change rapidly, he consulted a doctor who told him, "I don't understand how you could be standing here talking to me. You have an extremely low hemoglobin level of three. You should be dead."

By January 2010, the doctor told my friend that he had cancer of the blood. My friend replied, "I do not accept it! I cancel those words!" By the end of March, after several tests and a brief treatment, the doctor was pleasantly surprised to find him completely healed and told him to return in July. On his return, the doctor declared that he was in excellent health and requested to see him again every six months for the next two years. The doctor also said that if after two years, my friend continued to be healthy, he would close his case. When he heard this, my friend simply said, "When Jesus intervenes, He perfects all things. He never does anything halfway. Therefore, I am not worried. You can examine me as often as you please because I know that Jesus healed me and, for His glory, I will remain healed!"

In my friend's three testimonies, God's love for His children is clearly evident.

- **Jesus became sin and carried our sinful nature so we could be justified.**

    For He made Him who knew no sin to be sin for us, that we might become the righteousness of God in Him.
    (2 Corinthians 5:21)

- **Jesus died in our place so we can share in His eternal life.**

    But God demonstrates His own love toward us, in that while we were still sinners, Christ died for us.
    (Romans 5:8)

- **Jesus carried our curse so we could be blessed.**

    Christ has redeemed us from the curse of the law, having become a curse for us. (Galatians 3:13)

In light of these truths, I have seen many delivered. Jesus took all curses so we could receive the blessings.

During a night of miracles, a child was healed of a generational curse of astigmatism and myopia. The child was in Sunday school. When I called the children, he came running, and God instantly healed him. God is awesome!

- **Jesus paid for our poverty so we could be prosperous.**

    Yet for your sakes He became poor, that you through His poverty might become rich. (2 Corinthians 8:9)

- **Jesus suffered our shame so we could partake of His glory.**

    ...bringing many sons to glory.... (Hebrews 2:10)

- **Jesus suffered our rejection so we could be accepted in Him.**

Rejection is the most common emotional problem today, but thousands have been delivered in our deliverance sessions.

Rejection is one of the deepest wounds the human soul can experience, but Jesus suffered it on the cross.

How can we appropriate the benefits of the cross? By faith. Therefore, there are no substitutions for living by faith. We can trust in God's character and believe that He is righteous, just, and faithful and will keep all of His promises.

There are many examples I can share with you that would illustrate this point, but the one that touched me deeply is the testimony of a woman who grew up with a spirit of rejection that kept her from giving or receiving love. Furthermore, she was besieged by unforgiveness and bitterness against her parents. Her mother had traveled to the United States seeking a better future for her family, but, in the process, she had to leave behind her two-year-old daughter in the care of her father, a man who had no idea how to care for her due to his alcoholism. Knowing the circumstances in which she grew up, it is easy to see that love was scarce in this child's life. The feeling of abandonment caused her to find refuge in smoking, which enslaved her in the chains of addiction.

One day, now an adult, she visited our church and accepted Jesus as Lord and Savior and surrendered her life to Him. Instantly, God began to work wonders in her life. The first step in her inner healing was help for her to forgive her parents. Then, we had to rebuke the spirit of rejection and deliver her from her nicotine addiction. Once this was done, she received inner healing and deliverance. Today, she is living life to the fullest, serving in church, and is an excellent disciple of Christ.

...through whom also we have access by faith into this grace in which we stand. (Romans 5:2)

What Are the Benefits of the Cross?

- ## The cross delivered us from the "old man."

Our old man was crucified with Him.　　　(Romans 6:6)

The *"old man"* is our sinful Adamic nature, which can be summed up in one word: *rebellion*. We all carry a rebellious being within us. We were born this way because we were conceived and formed in iniquity. (See Psalm 51:5.) The only way to defeat this rebellious man is execution—a sentence that has already been carried out at the cross. This historic event is real and unchanging. Knowing and understanding this event will make you free.

- ## The cross delivered us from "self."

The ego is the part of the soul where the "self" dwells. It is where "I want" and "I think" can be found. Many people choose not to surrender to Jesus out of selfishness because they are afraid to leave their family, wealth, position, comfort, or sense of security.

---

*Ego is the greatest obstacle keeping us
from carrying out God's will.*

One manifestation of ego or self is egocentrism, or selfishness. This is equivalent to thinking that the world revolves around us. It is believing that we are the center of attention and that other people don't deserve to be appreciated or esteemed at the same level as we do. It also means that Jesus exists to please us, rather than our existing to please Him. A few manifestations of self or ego that need to be sacrificed are: pride, personal ambition, radical nationalism, sectarianism, and racism. What is the remedy for ego? The answer is the cross. Every ministry, man, or woman who fails to submit to the principle of the cross risks becoming corrupted. Therefore, you must decide to apply the cross to your ego. Otherwise, you will become a victim of the spirit of witchcraft, which uses ego to exercise dominion and lordship by force.

When you apply the cross to your ego, Satan cannot touch you. The cross is the only safe place to be. I know when a person is applying the cross to his ego because that person becomes humble in word and action.

On the other hand, many people live humbly, but without God's power. This happens when religion leads people to seek salvation through good works. Once more, let us remember that it is impossible to be holy by our own strength and discipline. We need the power and the grace of the cross.

The more I humble myself, the more power God manifests through me.

- **The cross delivered us from the flesh.**

Then [Jesus] said to them all, "If anyone desires to come after Me, let him deny himself, and take up his cross daily, and follow Me." (Luke 9:23)

The flesh always wants to act independently of God's will. The only requirement to live in the flesh is to do our own will. However, if we apply God's supernatural power to the flesh by accepting the work of the cross and obeying His Word, we will always live in victory.

- **The cross delivered us from the world.**

But God forbid that I should boast except in the cross of our Lord Jesus Christ, by whom the world has been crucified to me, and I to the world. (Galatians 6:14)

Most believers live under duress by the world's system—by its power, comfort, material rewards, fears, and anxieties.

The Bible commands us not to allow the world to mold us according to its standards. To avoid this, we must reject the worldly mentality and begin to renew our minds until we can think like God thinks. This does not require us to separate ourselves entirely from other people. God loves the world, but He hates the world's anti-God system. We must go into the world as lights and remove the veil from the eyes of those who live in darkness. We must not become like the world, but we need to be able to lead people to Christ.

- **The cross delivered us from Satan's power and authority.**

Having disarmed principalities and powers, He made a public spectacle of them, triumphing over them in it.
(Colossians 2:15)

On the cross, Jesus defeated the devil. This victory is irrevocable, eternal, and permanent. Satan cannot do anything to change it. If we come in contact with the enemy on any subject other than the cross, we can be defeated. But if we confront him at the cross, we will always be victorious. Again, Satan cannot change the work that was done at the cross. It is eternal. However, he can camouflage it and diminish its power, and that is the direction, or goal, of his strategies.

Battles come on a daily basis, but Jesus gives us the victory, as we can see in the following testimony.

Our church often encounters youth who need to be rescued from drug addiction and restored. This was precisely the case of a young man who was addicted to several different drugs, some of which he used as part of satanic rituals. After participating in these rituals, he would experience terrible bouts of anger, which scared even him. Thanks to God, at some point in his life, he began to understand that he needed help, and he visited our church in hopes of freeing himself from bondage.

My wife took over this case. For three days, she ministered deliverance to this young man with passion and perseverance until God's power delivered him from captivity! Today, we can testify that this young man has been totally set free, and he is a living testimony of unconditional service in the church. He is a new man. Undoubtedly, the Lord brought him to us with a purpose. He wanted this young man to be free of his bondage and free to serve Him.

When we take the path of the cross, we can expect many benefits, including deliverance, healing, and freedom of every kind of bondage.

What Message Should We Preach for the Power of God to Be Loosened?

We preach Christ crucified.　　　　　(1 Corinthians 1:23)

Many churches have substituted the message of the cross with other messages that neither transform nor edify the people, messages that are incapable of producing miracles because they lack power. We must return to the message of the cross. The church needs to know this truth.

The only message capable of loosening God's supernatural power is the message of the cross.

Why does God's power seem absent from many lives and ministries? Why are the sick not healed? Why do the blind not recover their sight? Why are the lame not walking? Why are we not seeing cancer dry up and disappear?

There is only one answer to these questions: because we are not preaching the message of the cross.

Because the foolishness of God is wiser than men, and the weakness of God is stronger than men.

　　　　　(1 Corinthians 1:25)

The cross is the true source of wisdom and power.

Without the power of the cross, we can teach good morals, practice good Christian ethics, have good intentions, and even preach good sermons, but we cannot produce a changed or transformed heart. Yet if we preach the message of the cross—Christ crucified and resurrected—we will see God's supernatural power confirmed with miracles, signs, and wonders. Jesus died, was raised from the dead, and defeated the enemy with power and authority in order to give us that same power, which He loosened at the cross. Let us continue His ministry on earth, expanding the kingdom of God throughout the world.

If you have never surrendered your life to Jesus, this is the moment for you to know the real, living, and resurrected Christ. The Word of God says that *"all have sinned and fall short of the glory of God"* (Romans 3:23), and that *"the wages of sin is death, but the gift of God is eternal life in Christ Jesus our Lord"* (Romans 6:23). Jesus came to die and shed His blood on the cross so that we could live. If you believe this is true, then please repeat this prayer:

> Heavenly Father, I recognize that I am a sinner. I repent of all my sins. I confess with my mouth that Jesus is the Son of God and that the Father raised Him from the dead. I am saved, healed, and delivered. I am a son/daughter of God, created in His image, to manifest His person and His power on this earth. Amen!

Summary

- The death of Jesus is divided into three parts: His physical death, His spiritual death, and His resurrection.

- Before Jesus died, He was whipped and beaten, His beard was plucked, He was spat upon, and He was made to wear a crown of thorns. Finally, He was crucified.

- Jesus fulfilled two roles on the cross: our priest and our sacrifice.

- The cross is the basis for God to provide absolute and total provision to mankind.

- The cross is the only true source of supernatural power.

- On the cross, Jesus loosened God's supernatural grace.

- When grace is set aside, one can easily become legalistic, which can lead to witchcraft and curses.

- The works of the cross are what the cross did *for* us and what the cross did *in* us.

- A divine exchange took place at the cross: Jesus took our wickedness and loosened His power and goodness.

- Faith is the way we appropriate the benefits of the cross.

- The cross delivered us from the flesh, self, the world, and Satan's power.

- The only message that loosens God's supernatural power is the message of the cross.

5

Faith: The First Dimension of the Supernatural

As the blood seeped from his body, an eighteen-year-old young man who had been stabbed seven times was loaded aboard a helicopter in a desperate attempt to save his life. On the way to the hospital, he cried out to God: "I know I have deeply hurt my family, friends, and people I have never even met. I might be responsible for the death of some people. I deserve what is happening to me, but please forgive me."

At age eleven, this young man had experienced the painful divorce of his parents. Although their marriage had appeared to be perfect on the outside, it had masked the hidden reality of abuse, rejection, and rebellion. Trying to escape his dysfunctional upbringing, this young man went to the streets, where eventually he was arrested after a fight that was provoked by excessive drinking. While at a party, gang members had begun to attack his friends. In trying to defend them, he had suffered his severe injuries. Immediately after crying out to God, however, he heard a doctor's voice saying, "You are okay. You are in the hospital." God had given him a new opportunity to live.

And yet, his life continued to spiral downward into even worse problems. Despite his many friends, his women, and his attempts at escape through illegal drugs, he could not escape the void in his life. He would cry bitterly because of the emptiness he felt. He wanted to change but didn't know how.

One day, he was invited to attend a House of Peace (our home fellowship groups). He only attended in an attempt to silence the persistent person who had been bugging him to attend. It was then that God began to speak to him. Eventually, he attended a youth service where he saw hundreds of young people praising God and crying out to Him. At first, he thought they looked ridiculous. As he was about to leave, someone took him by the hand and led him to the altar. Not understanding what was happening, he began to tremble. He heard the words of the youth pastor: "The Lord says, 'I know you have doubts about Me; you don't believe.'" As the youth pastor went on, the young man was stunned. Someone he had never met was talking about his life, about his relationship with his parents, about the bitterness he felt toward his mother, and about his relationship with a young woman. He began to cry like a child and he asked God to forgive him. At that instant, he surrendered his life. As he left the service, he felt the conviction that God is real. He also realized that despite everything he had ever done, God loved him. From that day forward, that young man's life changed. Today, he is full of love for his parents. God has filled the void in his life with faith in the supernatural.

The supernatural dimension is an eternal realm—invisible, permanent, and unchanging. It is where all things exist and are complete, the perennial "now" that can be accessed only by faith. If we want to know and move in the supernatural, we need revelation and understanding of the three dimensions. This is a fundamental requirement for receiving supernatural power from a supernatural God. The three dimensions of the supernatural are:

- Faith

- Anointing

- Glory

In the body of Christ, legitimate movements of the Holy Spirit have blessed thousands of people. In every move of the Spirit, there are always some who will take a truth to the extreme until it becomes a stronghold, then, a dogma, until, finally, it becomes a complete impediment to any move of the Spirit. Faith is one of those truths that can be misunderstood. Some people think they live by faith when, in truth, they are far from doing so. In many cases, faith has been reduced to something natural when it should be supernatural. With this in mind, I will begin by defining what faith is not.

Faith is not presumption or optimism. These things can resemble faith, but they are not faith.

What Is Faith?

Now faith is the substance of things hoped for, the evidence of things not seen.   (Hebrews 11:1)

The word *"faith"* is translated from the Hebrew word *emunah*, meaning "firmness, steadfastness, fidelity." As you can see, each of these meanings describes an aspect of God's nature. And they have nothing to do with presumption or optimism. The factor that assures us that the Lord will act is that God cannot lie or fail to keep His word. If He said it, you can rest assured that it will be as He said.

- **Faith is the mind of the Holy Spirit revealed to man so that he might operate and have dominion in this dimension of time, space, and matter.**

Now faith is the assurance (the confirmation, the title deed) of the things [we] hope for, being the proof of things [we] do not see and the conviction of their reality [faith perceiving as real fact what is not revealed to the senses].
                          (Hebrews 11:1 AMP)

A more literal translation from the Greek would be: "Now faith is the reality of the foundation where hope takes root, or is established. It is the reality of all that exists, and it exercises control and dominion over the things we cannot see."

Faith is the divine ability given to man to go beyond the natural realm. As I said earlier, if God had planned for man to live only in the natural dimension, He never would have given him faith. God created the natural realm. He dwells in and out of it, but He is not bound by it. God set time in motion, but when He created man, He placed a yearning for eternity within him, thereby enabling man to live in both dimensions—the natural and the supernatural. The invisible spiritual realm is superior to, and has dominion over, the natural realm.

The Natural Realm

Mankind attempts to define God according to the natural realm in which he lives, but God is much more than time, space, and matter. Our lives, circumstances, and problems are related to the natural dimension; therefore, the breakthrough will come when we begin to operate by faith.

> *Do not be conformed to this world (this age), [fashioned after and adapted to its external, superficial customs].*
> (Romans 12:2 AMP)

For us, the natural realm is reality, but in God's mind, this dimension is subject to being cursed. Nature is devastated by the curse that was put upon it after the fall and cries out for God's children to manifest the supernatural. We cannot get comfortable in one dimension that is always changing. Our faith needs absolute, unchanging values, like Jesus, His kingdom, and His Word.

*Everything to which you conform
will become your reality.*

What Is the Difference between the Natural and Supernatural Realms?

The spiritual realm is eternal and permanent, and it operates in the perennial "now," or continuous present. To better understand this concept, let us differentiate between the natural dimension and eternity. The natural dimension is like a straight line that has a beginning and an end. Eternity is a circle; it has neither a beginning nor an end. When you enter eternity, everything is. This is God's habitat, where time does not exist. However, He always speaks to existence from the eternal realm.

> *For thus says the High and Lofty One who inhabits eternity.* (Isaiah 57:15)

Faith allows us to cross the limits of the natural realm and to reach eternity. We must decide which realm we want to inhabit: the realm of time or the realm of eternity. If we walk in the spiritual dimension, we will, in the natural, receive all the benefits Jesus provided at the cross. In the spiritual realm, everything is finished and complete: health, deliverance, prosperity, salvation, strength, peace, and all other material, emotional, and spiritual provision we might need on earth. Everything was provided for by Jesus at the cross. How can we manifest these things on earth? The only way to do it is by faith.

What Does the Natural Realm Represent?

The visible realm represents our surroundings. Therefore, we need a breakthrough in order to cross over the barriers of time, space, and matter and exit our natural realm, in which time has enslaved us. We need to be free of the bondage that keeps us subject to the senses—free, so we do not have to smell, feel, taste, hear, or see to believe. When we understand faith, the impossible becomes possible because faith has dominion and control over the laws of time, space, and matter. For example, when we go to refinance our house, the bank establishes that it will take thirty years to finish paying off the mortgage. Due to interest on the loan, by the end of those thirty years, we will have paid four times the value of the house. In this case, the one who determined the time to complete payments on the house was the bank. But what if we determine the time by exercising our faith and paying off the mortgage in only five years? Then, by faith, we allow God to supernaturally bring into the natural realm the resources we need to keep us from being enslaved by a debt for a longer period of time. In other words, we allow God to deliver His divine provision. If we do this, we break the laws of time. We submit to the provision, not the debt!

I make my plans according to faith, not according to time. For instance, the bank financed the mortgage on my house for thirty years, but I believed that God would pay off that loan in only five years. One year ago, I declared, "Lord, I am believing that my house is going to be paid off within the next five years. God, I don't want to live under debt, so I am asking You to pay off my house." A few months ago, a "spiritual son" of mine from Brazil came to me and said, "Pastor, I just had a business deal close, and the Lord put it on my heart to pay off your house." This man is not exceptionally wealthy. I had never told him about this matter, nor had I asked him to do this. He was following the Lord's direction. And, in that moment, what I had believed came to pass. Most people live only according to time. When the bank says it is going to take thirty years to pay off your house, you believe it and plan accordingly. But if you plan according to the spiritual realm and not according to the natural realm, you will be able to break the laws of time.

Here is another example. When the doctor says, "Your cancer is hereditary. Your grandparents had it, your parents had it, and now you have it. All you can do is undergo an expensive and painful treatment," it is time for a decision. Do you break the curse and operate by faith to receive your healing? Or, do you believe only the doctor and wait for his prognosis to mature? In such cases, your greatest hope is to appropriate what Jesus did on the cross and begin to live by faith.

When God spoke to me about building our current church home with a seating capacity of six thousand, every contractor said it would take no less than five years to finish. I, however, believed God when He told me that it would be completed in less than three years. God provided the finances and gathered the right people, and the building was finished in twenty-eight months, within the time I had believed. Once again, this is an example of how faith can break the laws of time! If it happened to me, it can happen to you. The only thing you need to do is decide to live by faith and not by sight.

You might think, *That is easy for you to say because God has blessed you with gifts, grace, and favor.* Of course He has, but let me tell you that my beginning was just like yours. When God spoke to me about a new building for six thousand people, He also said it would be done debt free. When I received an estimate of the cost, I had to stretch my faith because the total cost, including land, materials, and labor, was close to twenty-five million dollars. In that moment, when the Holy Spirit gave me the order to begin construction, I had only faith, not money. This had a great impact in our area because this type of project had never been done, much less in the Hispanic community. But we obeyed God and started construction with only seven hundred thousand dollars in the bank, which was barely enough to cover the cost of the steel beams. Yet God, through His prophets, confirmed what He had already said to me. It was then that I received what I call a *rhema* word from Him. A prophecy is a word from God concerning the future, but a *rhema* word from God is for today, right now. That *rhema* word included a biblical promise that kept me strong throughout the construction process:

> *For thus says the LORD God of Israel: "The bin of flour shall not be used up, nor shall the jar of oil run dry."*
> (1 Kings 17:14)

This verse became a reality for me. In order to keep construction moving forward, we needed to come up with approximately five hundred thousand dollars each month. I had to believe for that amount every month. Over the next twenty-eight months, we fully experienced a level of God's faithfulness that went beyond human logic. He never failed us. On several occasions, we owed as much as eight hundred thousand dollars but had only fifty thousand in the bank account just five days before it was due. But God was faithful and provided all of the twenty-five million dollars in construction costs in less than three years. Living by faith, we built our church debt free, and God did not use millionaires to do it. The biggest gift we ever received was twenty-five thousand dollars. The rest came from the united effort of a faithful people whom God blessed so they could give. He used office workers, laborers, professionals, youth, and housewives—common folks like you and me. He did it this way so that we could announce to the four winds that He is our provider, so that His name would be glorified.

If He did this for us, He can do it for anyone who is willing to believe in Him. This has served as our powerful testimony: when God says something and we believe it, we can consider it a done deal. Today, many of our spiritual children and even other pastors have taken this testimony as an example to build their temples debt free. God is doing it. Praise the Lord!

- **Faith is now.**

When is faith due? Faith is now! Faith is the past and the future together in the present, constituting the now.

And God said to Moses, "I AM WHO I AM."   (Exodus 3:14)

God does not need time. He dwells in the *now*. He does not need the day or the night to do His works because the supernatural realm—the past and the future—come together in the present. From God's standpoint, His future can invade the present. One reason we do not see supernatural manifestations—miracles, signs, and wonders—in the church is that these things take place in the *now*, while we live our lives waiting for things to happen in the future. Many men and women of God speak in the future tense. They say that God will bring a revival, will perform great miracles, and will visit us with His glory. They use a language for the future, not the *now*. Faith is now! We can believe that God is bringing a revival now and is performing miracles now! The harvest of souls is greater than it has ever been in the history of the church. It is ready for gathering—now! Faith compresses time. Therefore, what would normally take a year can now be done in one day. Everything works according to our faith.

Faith is God's radar in the believer to determine the distance and time between the natural and supernatural, the visible and invisible.

You will also declare a thing, and it will be established for you; so light will shine on your ways.   (Job 22:28)

One day, I was praying at home before one of our worship services, and the Holy Spirit said to me, *If My people believe My Word, no spirit of infirmity can touch them.* I believed it and taught it in the service, where many miracles took place.

On another occasion, I was asked to pray for a baby who was born with a collapsed pulmonary system, cerebral hemorrhage, and retinopathy, which left the child in danger of going blind. All these problems were the result of an incorrect oxygen level administered at birth. During his short life, he had already received five blood transfusions and, according to the doctors, was to remain hospitalized until they could be satisfied of his progress. So, I prayed for the baby, declaring that what is impossible for men is possible for God.

A week later, the doctors released the baby from the hospital because he was completely healed. All his organs were perfectly normal, as if nothing negative had ever happened. In this case, science had to testify of the baby's healing because the doctors had proof of this child's "before" and his "after." What had happened? Through prayer with the child's mother, we had activated our faith and compressed time. We had surpassed the natural laws and activated God's supernatural power over her baby.

Faith is not in the future because faith is not going to be; faith is now.

Most believers know where they came from. Some know where they are going. But few believe what they are *now.* They are unaware of what God is doing and saying *now.* When we abandon faith to live according to sight only, the enemy makes us focus on the problems, infirmities, and difficulties. But let us remember that these things are temporary; by faith, they are passing away and dying each second. Sickness is passing. Poverty is passing. Oppression and depression are passing. By faith, we must believe that God is intervening *now.*

Now is the time to activate our faith. Right now, let's declare and establish the time and distance to receive healing for cancer or any other sickness we might have. Let's declare the money we need and when it will appear supernaturally. Let's declare a time—three or five days, you decide—in which God will do the miracle. We must determine the time, and God will do it. He said we were healed and prosperous. I'm not suggesting that we order God around like a trained dog or a servant. I'm saying that these things are already done in the supernatural, and they are waiting for us to decide when we will claim them. Things in the spirit *are*; they are complete. God's name is *"I AM WHO I AM."* (Exodus 3:14). He placed in us the ability to determine the distance between the visible and invisible realms. When we speak, there is matter—raw material—in our mouths to create by His Word and to activate by faith.

> *Now faith is the substance of things hoped for, the evidence of things not seen.* (Hebrews 11:1)

The Definition of Faith Is in the Now

If we take this definition of faith, we will begin to see things as God sees them.

> *I am God, and there is none like Me, declaring the end from the beginning, and from ancient times things that are not yet done.* (Isaiah 46:9–10)

God declares the end from the beginning. How, then, do we get to the *now*? In our culture, we are used to seeing things from a linear, logical standpoint. In other words, to get to the end, we must start at the beginning. However, God finishes something before showing men the beginning. In other words, nothing exists in this world until it has been finished by God.

When faith touches things that cannot be seen, it gives us conviction and persuades us to wait for them. Faith converts things that cannot be seen into something certain, something real. This happens in the *now,* not in the future. If we read the definition of faith in a logical way, we will notice that there is still something pending, something that has yet to manifest, something that waits for the future. But remember that in eternity, God already did it. He has already formed new organs and bones. He has already healed incurable diseases and performed creative miracles. What is our part in all of this? All we need to do is appropriate the miracle by faith, *now*!

I am challenging you to activate your faith to believe for miracles that appear impossible. Allow me to remind you that nothing is impossible for God. (See Matthew 19:26.) Please read this testimony, which will bolster your faith:

This miracle occurred in the midst of a normal church service while I taught the congregation on the fact that faith is for now. Among those in attendance was a woman who had suffered with bad knees for the past fifteen years. Doctors had told her that her ligaments and cartilage were destroyed, causing her chronically intense pain. They had told her to seek surgical repair as soon as possible.

On this particular Sunday, this woman held on to her faith and decided to believe God and His promises found in the Bible. She said, "I have been taught that faith is for tomorrow, but I take it now. Today, God creates in me two new knees." In that moment, God's power descended and created something new. No one touched her. Suddenly, she felt the impulse to run to the altar. As she did, she felt no pain whatsoever; she just ran. What took place here was not a healing of her bad knees but the miraculous creation of two brand-new knees. This is how God's supernatural power operates!

> *Being confident of this very thing, that He who has begun a good work in you will complete it until the day of Jesus Christ.* (Philippians 1:6)

God started creating us in eternity and finished us before giving us the shape and form we have today. We arrived in the *now* via God's faith. Therefore, we don't have to seek faith, because God already gave it to us to receive all that He promised. We will believe what we can't see only if we see it through the faith of the One who sees. God sees our healing, prosperity, and happiness because He already did it all.

- **Faith feeds on impossibilities.**

A believer full of God's supernatural faith is passionate about the impossible, and his faith is fed when he confronts "impossible" situations. When God gave each one of us a measure of faith, an appetite for the impossible came into our spirits. We were created to have this appetite for the impossible.

- **Faith perceives as real that which has yet to be revealed to the natural senses.**

The nature of faith is not to be revealed to the senses. When God commands that we do something, it might not make sense, because, if it did, it would not be supernatural. The carnal mind cannot see the invisible. To the mind, it is as if it did not exist.

- **God gave each person a measure of faith.**

> *God has dealt to each one a measure of faith.* (Romans 12:3)

The Word confirms that everyone has faith but not in the same measure. God will take those who have believed for greater things to a higher level of faith. When we take our measure of faith to the limit, God takes us to a higher level. It is possible to lose that measure of faith instead of gaining more if we choose to remain comfortable at a place where our faith is not challenged. If we are being good stewards with the measure of faith we have, God will give us more.

What is a measure of faith? What does Scripture say about this? A measure of faith is the sphere of influence and the level of authority where we place our faith to produce. It is my firm belief that one human being is capable of influencing—for good or evil—an average of around ten thousand people in his or her lifetime.

The Level of Authority

In the spirit realm, everything operates according to levels of authority. For instance, each person receives a measure of authority in the church, and his or her measure of faith is to be used effectively according to his or her level of authority. Remember, if our measure of faith is sufficient to move mountains or destroy strongholds, our level of authority will be proportionate to that measure.

Because everyone was given a measure of faith, there will never be an excuse not to believe in God.

How Do We Receive God's Faith?

So Jesus answered and said to them, "Have faith in God." (Mark 11:22)

A more literal translation for this verse is, "Have God's faith." In Greek, the verb is in the passive voice, which means that the action comes from outside. In other words, Jesus does not ask us to have faith in God, but God gives us a measure of faith that belongs to Him. In other words, our human nature is incapable of generating faith on its own. We must take hold of God's faith.

Human nature can doubt but not believe;
divine nature can believe but not doubt.

In essence, Jesus was telling Peter, "Receive God's faith to bless others." Later, in Acts, we see Peter saying the same thing.

Then Peter said, "Silver and gold I do not have, but what I do have I give you: In the name of Jesus Christ of Naza-reth, rise up and walk." (Acts 3:6)

Every member of our church has been trained through discipleship groups and our Leadership Institute to exercise his or her God-given measure of faith. This includes those who are just starting out in the gospel. Here is a testimony that illustrates what I have just stated:

A House of Peace, led by a young married couple who had joined the church only six months prior, was visited by a couple who had been diagnosed with AIDS. The leader's wife stood with authority and prayed with faith, asking God to heal them. When the visiting couple returned to the doctor to be retested, their results came back negative. Medically speaking, AIDS continues to be an incurable disease that attacks the immune system, decreasing the body's ability to fight infection. To God, however, this disease has already been abolished from the face of the earth. What seems impossible to man is possible for God!

The power of God in the realm
of miracles is called faith.

Let's study this in more detail:

• **God gave Abraham "dynamite" faith.**

[Abraham] *did not waver at the promise of God through unbelief, but was strengthened [endynamoo] in faith, giving glory to God.* (Romans 4:20)

Abraham's faith needed strengthening. *Endynamoo*—or God's "dynamite"—had to come upon him. As a human being, Abraham did not have the faith he needed. Therefore, God had to fill him with His faith to help him wait for the son God promised. When God finished strengthening Abraham, he was persuaded and convicted to wait for the certainty of his *now*. God wants to do the same with us. He wants to use "dynamite" to blow apart our doubt and unbelief and to fill us with His faith to receive the miracles He has prepared for us.

[Abraham was] *fully convinced that what He had promised He was also able to perform.* (Romans 4:21)

When we are totally convinced and persuaded, nothing will make us waver or doubt. Regardless of what people say, the symptoms we have, or the circumstances we are experiencing, we will know that these things do not change what God promised. Some people doubt that God's promises will come to pass because they are not fully convinced or persuaded. No one can be fully convinced while doubting.

When we have God's faith, His Word in our mouths is the same as it is in His mouth.

- **God used "dynamite" in Sarah's womb.**

  By faith Sarah herself also received strength [dynamis] to conceive seed, and she bore a child when she was past the age, because she judged Him faithful who had promised. (Hebrews 11:11)

Sarah needed to receive *dynamis*—God's dynamite—for her womb to become fruitful. When God told her that she would have a son at her advanced age, she laughed (see Genesis 18:12), but when He gave her His "dynamite" faith, her infertility was transformed into fruitfulness. Likewise, many people today are sterile. They don't know how to bear fruit in their personal lives, marriages, or finances. Some ministries are also stuck, unable to grow or bear the desired fruit. They need to be transformed by God's dynamite faith.

How Do We Receive God's Faith?

God's faith to believe as He believes is received by saying, "Lord, I open my heart so You can fill it with Your dynamite faith. Destroy in me all doubt, unbelief, reasoning, and argumentation so that I may receive the miracles You promised me, and so that I may give to others the faith You have imparted into my life."

My friend, God wants to give us dynamite faith today and make us fruitful so we can pray for the sick and see them healed. We can deliver the captives and give sight to the blind. We can open deaf ears and call the lame to walk. When God gives us His dynamite faith, and we are persuaded to use it, it is not time to remain still but to take action.

What Are the Enemies of Faith?

Every day, we battle enemies of faith, but sometimes we don't realize what or who they are because we don't recognize them.

- **Unbelief**

  Beware, brethren, lest there be in any of you an evil heart of unbelief in departing from the living God.
  (Hebrews 3:12)

Unbelief is a wicked spirit that uses reason to make us refuse or oppose God. Unbelief is everywhere, even in some pulpits, where messages are delivered that feed further unbelief, conformity, and religiosity. We are surrounded by a hostile world that opposes God. The world's objective is to develop unbelief. In addition, we now have to deal with "educated unbelief." What does this mean? Educated unbelief tries to supplant the spiritual man. To accomplish this, scientific, philosophical, and psychological arguments are developed for the sole purpose of eliminating faith. Unbelief has become the means through which we measure our reality—what seems possible and what seems impossible. We must be delivered from unbelief!

The only biblical reason to fail is unbelief.

Truth is the highest level of reality, and it may be understood only by revelation—Jesus is truth. When God speaks, what He says is truth, and it will come to pass, regardless of circumstances or what theologians, doctors, or the devil may say. God exists in the realm of truth; His name is The Great I Am. God is the same yesterday, today, and forever. (See Hebrews 13:8.)

Truth is the highest level of reality.

- **Human reason**

By faith we understand that the worlds were framed.
(Hebrews 11:3)

"By faith we understand." Note that faith comes first and then understanding. To believe God with human reasoning doesn't make sense, and it will never increase our level of faith. The enemy's goal is to keep us within the limits of reason, as he did to Eve in the garden of Eden. This is why, each time we seek to understand God through reason, we once again eat of the tree of the knowledge of good and evil.

When I say that reason is the enemy of faith, or the supernatural, it is because I want us to understand a very important point: reason, or intellect, has its place and should be used in the physical world to make wise decisions in the natural realm. God gave us the ability to reason for a specific purpose. Therefore, it is good to use reason within the natural realm. However, if we try using it in the spiritual realm, it will not work. When

I say this, I am affirming that reason is the enemy of faith but also confirming that it is the ability given by God to operate in the natural realm.

> ## *Faith is the ability given to every believer to believe the unreasonable.*

Reason never stands on the side of faith. When reason is in effect, it separates us from faith. This is why much of what God did, as recorded in the Bible, appears unreasonable to human reason. Let us look at the following examples:

- **Shadrach, Meshach, and Abed-Nego were cast into the fire but not burned.**

  "Look!" he answered, "I see four men loose, walking in the midst of the fire; and they are not hurt, and the form of the fourth is like the Son of God."   (Daniel 3:25)

By human reasoning, it doesn't make sense that while the king cast three people into the fire, four people appeared to be walking in the midst of it. Also, it doesn't make sense that no one got burned in a fire that was at the highest possible temperature.

- **Abraham fathered his descendants in his old age.**

  No longer shall your name be called Abram, but your name shall be Abraham; for I have made you a father of many nations.   (Genesis 17:5)

Trying to reason that a ninety-nine-year-old man and his barren ninety-year-old wife conceived a child is impossible. This can be understood only by faith.

- **Noah built an ark.**

  By faith Noah, being divinely warned of things not yet seen, moved with godly fear, prepared an ark for the saving of his household, by which he condemned the world

*and became heir of the righteousness which is according
to faith.* (Hebrews 11:7)

A miracle took place when animals began to arrive from all
over the world. Tigers came from Siberia and India, elephants
from India, lions from Africa, and kangaroos from Australia.
It was a miracle that many of these animals traveled in pairs
according to species. It was a miracle that these wild animals
coexisted peacefully within the ark for forty days without attacking each other. This can be understood only by faith.

In the absence of reason, faith says, "Now." In the presence of faith, God acts now.

Faith cannot be judged or proven in a court of law where reason rules because there are no books or codes that can judge
faith. Jurisprudence judges on the basis of human reasoning
and deals only with facts, tangible acts that can be proven on
the basis of our five natural senses—sight, smell, taste, hearing, and touch. A court of law has no room for faith.

If a doctor diagnoses a sickness, even when God's Word says
we are healed, the human verdict will most often be sickness because this deals with two different realms: the natural and the
supernatural. The more time we spend trying to reason what
God wants to do in and through us, the more we will lose the
manifestation of the supernatural—His miracles and blessings.

During one particular service, God placed in my heart a di-
rective to call forth women who were barren or unable to conceive. Among the great number of women who came to the altar
was a woman who had had her fallopian tubes tied years prior,
making it impossible for her to have more children. During that
service, God was glorified in this woman. The following month,
she became pregnant. God did a wonderfully creative miracle in
her. He gave her a brand-new reproductive system, including new
fallopian tubes. The miracle was even more amazing because the
doctor later confirmed the miracle by doing an ultrasound that

found reproductive organs where there had been none. In the meantime, her baby was growing and in perfect condition. The doctor expected the birth to be on time. Several months later, this woman rejoiced at the arrival of her beautiful gift from God. A precious baby boy came into this world as a demonstration of God's supernatural power to procreate. In our ministry, we often see women who were told by medical doctors that they could not have children activate their faith and become pregnant.

No Bible story makes sense until God comes on the scene.

Renewing our minds is a process by which we substitute God's logic for our human reason. Only then are we able to realize that everything He does makes sense. Preachers and teachers of the Word are called to make certain that unbelief does not take root in the hearts and minds of those who hear them.

In the absence of reason, all things are possible. When faith is present, even the impossible is made possible.

How to Cross Over from Reason to Faith

To live by faith, we must disconnect our reasoning ability and "loose" our minds. If we believe our minds, we will believe only in man-made reason and will doubt God's power. Faith doesn't need human reasoning to believe because it supersedes reasoning and is not based on common sense. Reasoning can become a mortal weapon against us when it causes us to explain why we are sick, impoverished, depressed, or experiencing marital problems, or when we have unforgiveness, bitterness, addictions, or sin. Hence the importance of rising to a higher dimension of faith.

The realm of the impossible is founded on human logic and established in human reason.

How Do We Rise from One Dimension of Faith to a Greater One?

For in [the gospel] *the righteousness of God is revealed from faith to faith; as it is written, "The just shall live by faith."* (Romans 1:17)

To go *"from faith to faith"* is to go from one dimension of faith to another. This indicates that the movement does not begin at the point of departure, but it takes off from a place already advanced. In other words, it is a movement that takes us from one level of faith to a greater degree of faith. The key to advance is the revelation, or revealed knowledge, of God. This is why faith and knowledge always go together. Therefore, when a person lacks revealed knowledge, it is impossible for that person to move to the next level of faith. On the other hand, when revelation is present, there is faith that catapults the individual into a new dimension.

The level of revelation in an individual determines the measure of faith in which he will operate.

If revealed knowledge ceases, faith also ceases. It will decelerate and enter into the natural realm. We cannot believe in something we do not know. This means that we cannot allow faith to become stagnant. Faith must be in constant movement; we must go from faith to faith. The same can be said about glory. We must go from glory to glory. (See 2 Corinthians 3:18.) We cannot become stagnant. The Christian life was never designed to stay at one level. We are always changing from glory to glory and from faith to faith.

In the testimony of a King Jesus daughter church in Orlando, Florida, we can see how God first leads us to believe in something that, in turn, propels our faith to believe for greater blessings.

A woman had been attending church for eight months when she was touched by God's power. She had been diagnosed with cancer of the uterus and had undergone surgery to have it removed. A friend told her that she should take advantage of the fact that I would be preaching in Orlando and to go to the church where I could pray for her, and she agreed to go. I did not see her, but God knew she was there. According to her testimony, while I ministered, I passed by her and said, "The Lord already healed on this side." She believed the words I spoke. However, in addition to the already mentioned problem, this woman had been diagnosed with congenital adrenal hyperplasia, a condition that impedes the kidneys from functioning properly, and obstructive sleep apnea, which caused her to fall asleep anywhere. All these conditions were causing problems in her relationships, but the process through which the Lord wanted to take her to exercise her faith did not end there. Several Sundays later, through a satellite transmission, I called forth people who were involved in fornication. This woman recognized her sin—she had been living with a man for fifteen years without being married to him. That was the key that loosened everything. As soon as she got married, she experienced her menstrual cycle, which had stopped three years prior due to the removal of her cancerous uterus. Without her uterus, she could not get pregnant. She dreamed of someday giving her husband a son, but, according to medical science, she had no hope. Yet the Lord manifested His great love in her life and gave her the miracle she was desperately looking for. After her wedding ceremony, she received the creative miracle of a new uterus and soon became pregnant. Today, she can drive without the fear of falling asleep and is overjoyed that her marriage is strong. She serves the Lord wholeheartedly.

If our faith is not kept active, nothing will happen. Is it possible to be stuck in a dimension of faith? Yes, it is possible, and there are clear signs that show when our faith has become inactive. For example, when nothing new happens in church, when the congregation ceases to grow, when signs, miracles, and wonders cease, or when God's presence is nowhere to be found, our faith has stopped growing. He wants us to advance to a greater level, but for that to happen, we need revelation to pave the way to a new dimension. If we want to walk in the *now*, we cannot ignore God's revelation for this time. We cannot walk in the present truth with yesterday's revelation because faith is *now*, always in the present.

To have faith in the now, we must have a revelation of the present truth.

You know and are established in the present truth.
(2 Peter 1:12)

Truth is present, and faith is *now*. If yesterday's faith were sufficient, the Bible would not command that we go *"from faith to faith."* God wants to do something new and fresh *now*! Faith has an expiration date. If it is not *now*, it is not faith. Furthermore, yesterday's revelation is worthless when we try to activate it now. What used to work no longer works. Therefore, God motivates us to take up a new dimension and revelation.

In conclusion, if you feel that your faith is inactive, this is the time to decide to go to another dimension with God. There, you will find something new and fresh—miracles, healing, and all types of provision. Now is the time to tell God, "Give me a new revelation that will take me to another dimension of faith. Connect me with men and women who can loosen it, so I can become like Peter, blessing the people, praying for the sick, and tending to people who need a touch of Your supernatural power." If we want to move in that dimension, we must start by understanding faith, which will give us access to the supernatural of God.

Summary

- Faith is not presumption, hope, or optimism.

- Faith is God's mind revealed to man and the divine ability to overcome the natural realm.

- There is conflict between reason and faith because they belong to two different realms: reason is temporal and faith is eternal.

- Faith is *now,* the past and the future united in the present.

- All believers have faith but in different measures—spheres of influence and levels of authority—that increase when they are exercised.

- In the realm of miracles, the power of God is called faith, and we need to receive it in dynamite proportions in order to bring forth the supernatural in the natural.

- The enemies of faith are unbelief and reason.

- The key to moving from one dimension of faith to another is God's revelation.

6

The Anointing: The Second Dimension of the Supernatural

The previous chapter covered the first of the three dimensions that make up the supernatural. Now, let us learn about the anointing. As I've already explained, to understand these dimensions constitutes the basis for loosening God's supernatural power. In this chapter, I will cover only a few specific points on the anointing.

What Is the Anointing?

The anointing is the ability God gives the believer to accomplish the work of the ministry and to serve Him. The physical act of anointing is to apply oil on someone for the purpose of consecrating the work of God in his or her life. It is a confirmation of a calling or function, sealed by the Holy Spirit, in which the oil is only a visible symbol. The person who anoints another is God's agent. This person applies the oil, but God is the One who sends His Holy Spirit. Since the earliest of times, anointing has been the way to seal the consecration of God on people who are called to carry out special functions, for example, kings and priests. Through the act of anointing, the person is enabled to carry out the assigned functions.

The anointing is God doing His work through our humanity.

There are different aspects of God's power, and their names vary according to the area in which they operate.

What Is Power Called in the Area of Ministry?

In the area of ministry, supernatural power is called the *holy anointing*.

> *I have found My servant David; with My holy oil I have*
> *anointed him.*   (Psalm 89:20)

In the Old Testament, the anointing was only a shadow of what we know of it today through the new covenant. Today, a variety of oils are used for the purpose of anointing, but with Moses, God gave specific instructions on how to prepare the oil of the holy anointing:

> *Also take for yourself quality spices—five hundred shek-*
> *els of liquid myrrh, half as much sweet-smelling cinna-*
> *mon (two hundred and fifty shekels), two hundred and*
> *fifty shekels of sweet-smelling cane, five hundred shekels*
> *of cassia, according to the shekel of the sanctuary, and*
> *a hin of olive oil. And you shall make from these a holy*
> *anointing oil, an ointment compounded according to the*
> *art of the perfumer. It shall be a holy anointing oil.*
> (Exodus 30:23–25)

God specified which ingredients to use, each representing a prophetic symbol of something that was to come in the New Testament.

- **Myrrh**

Myrrh is a bitter herb with a sweet aroma. It represents suffering, pain, anguish, distress, death, trials, tribulations, and persecution. Myrrh represents the price we pay for the anointing. Many desire the anointing but are not willing to pay the price to have it.

I have suffered...that I may know Him and the power of His resurrection, and the fellowship of His sufferings, being conformed to His death.   (Philippians 3:8, 10)

- **Cinnamon**

Cinnamon represents firmness and stability. These elements are applied to Christian character and are fundamental to operating in the anointing.

- **Cane**

Cane, or calamus in the King James Version, is a long, straight reed with green and red coloring that smells a bit like ginger. It is associated with the gifts of the Holy Spirit and divine authority. This is indicative of the anointing flowing in us when we submit to authority.

- **Cassia**

Cassia is a sweet-smelling bush of yellow flowers. The leaves of this plant are dried and pulverized to prepare the anointing oil. The word *cassia* derives from a root word that means "to bow down out of honor and reverence." Therefore, the cassia flower represents prayer, praise, and worship. It is said that its anointing generates the desire to pray and to worship God.

- **Oil**

The oil for the anointing is extracted from the olive tree, and it represents the Holy Spirit. The anointing has two important characteristics: it is a tangible substance that can be applied with a cloth or by pouring from a pot or jar, and it is transferable from one person to another.

The following testimony confirms the fact that the anointing can accumulate on objects and be transferred between people:

Not long ago, I took my car to the mechanic for routine maintenance. At the shop, there was a mechanic who was suffering with intense pain due to kidney stones. The shop's owner, knowing of my ministry and that my car was being serviced, told the mechanic to sit in the driver's seat and rub the keys of my car over the area of his pain. The instant this man rubbed my keys on his back, he felt the sudden urge to use the bathroom. When he returned, he held in his hands all the kidney stones that he had just passed. His pain was completely gone.

Now, understand that objects such as car keys have no healing power in and of themselves, but the anointing of God can accumulate on any object with the power to perform miracles.

What Was the Purpose of the Oil of the Holy Anointing?

In the Jewish temple, the oil of the holy anointing was used to anoint the tabernacle, the holy utensils, and the priests so that they could be consecrated, identified, and prepared to enter into God's presence.

With it you shall anoint the tabernacle of meeting and the ark of the Testimony. (Exodus 30:26)

In the tabernacle, no one could touch an instrument or utensil unless he had been anointed because the anointing is what prepares an individual to stand safely in God's presence. This is also true for us today. God first anoints us with His holy anointing and then consecrates and sanctifies us in preparation to receive His glory.

What Is the Difference between Talent and Anointing?

Many people trust and depend solely on their talents. Thus, when they praise, worship, and serve God, they do not do so wholeheartedly. Doing these things has nothing to do with talent but with how anointed one is. I have seen people with little talent bring God's presence like no one else when they praise.

I believe gifts and talents are needed, but we must learn to depend completely on the anointing of the Holy Spirit.

The anointing of the Holy Spirit is a deposit to receive God's glory.

In Him you also...were sealed with the Holy Spirit of promise. (Ephesians 1:13)

In the previous chapter, we learned that the Bible makes several references to the measure of our faith. I clarified that the measure of faith relates to the sphere of influence and the level of authority we have. Thus, it is necessary for our society to join the measures and gifts of each individual in order to operate at a greater level of power. We need each other. I need your measure—your sphere of influence and authority—and you need mine. When the measures and the gifts unite, God's glory descends. Otherwise, His glory will not come.

- **Personal anointing**

  But to each one of us grace was given according to the measure of Christ's gift. (Ephesians 4:7)

  Personal anointing is the measure of supernatural grace that God gives each believer to enable him or her to fulfill his or her calling—for example, personal anointing for business, to restore families, to perform miracles, or perhaps governmental, ministerial, or prophetic anointing.

- **Corporate anointing**

  ...till we all come to the unity of the faith and of the knowledge of the Son of God, to a perfect man, to the measure of the stature of the fullness of Christ. (Ephesians 4:13)

  A corporate anointing is an anointing of the Holy Spirit that is poured out when everyone present becomes as one in

Christ. When this happens, we see Christ operating through the church with miracles, signs, and wonders. This anointing is a thousand times stronger and more powerful than the personal anointing. Thus, God always commands us to seek unity and depend on one another, according to our measures, in order to become powerful on earth, just as Jesus is. Another term often used instead of anointing is the word *mantle*.

What Is a Mantle?

The word *mantle* has several meanings, including "a loose sleeveless garment worn over other clothes...a figurative cloak symbolizing preeminence or authority." It also refers to "the part of the interior of a terrestrial planet and especially the earth that lies beneath the crust and above the central core." In all its meanings, the mantle represents a covering, or protection.

The mantle, or anointing, is our covering while we reside on earth.

In the spiritual realm, the word *mantle* also means "glory, kindness, lordship, excellence, nobility, authority, strength, essence, and great courage."

The Two Mantles of Jesus

- **The mantle of His deity, which is His glory**

    Christ Jesus,...being in the form of God, did not consider it robbery to be equal with God, but made Himself of no reputation. (Philippians 2:5–7)

Before coming to earth, Jesus took off His mantle of glory. However, throughout the gospel of John, we read of seven miraculous signs that confirmed His identity as God's Son. The Father personally testified of His deity. He came like any other man, anointed by the Holy Spirit but without His mantle of glory, which He had willingly left behind in heaven.

- **The mantle of His humanity, which is His anointing**

For He whom God has sent speaks the words of God, for God does not give the Spirit by measure. (John 3:34)

What can we learn from this? That Jesus defeated the devil and his demons in the form of a common man but with the anointing of the Holy Spirit. With His anointing, He healed the sick, blind, and deaf; He rebuked demons; and He raised the dead—not as God but as a Man full of the Holy Spirit. If Jesus did this, we can do it, too. As a matter of fact, Jesus promised that we would do greater things than He! (See John 14:12.)

The anointing comes from God to man, but impartation is given from one man to another by God's will.

Some have great anointing but no ability to impart it to others. This is probably due to their inability to see beyond themselves or their ministries. It is also possible that, under an apostolic and prophetic ministry, because of faith, people receive the impartation of all types of gifts. Either way, the key to receiving a mantle is to have an open heart.

In the 1950s and 60s, God raised up men and women with the goal of bringing forth a great revival through healing, miracles, signs, and wonders. Most of them, however, never realized that the anointing and grace they received was to teach, train, and equip the church for future generations. They used them but rarely transferred or imparted their mantles to others so their ministries could continue for future generations. We admire those generals of God. Unfortunately, the anointing that came upon them often died with them because they failed to teach the church to flow in the same supernatural power, as Jesus did with His disciples.

Impartation takes place due to a direct intervention of the Holy Spirit. He takes the gift of one individual and gives a measure to others who desperately seek it. Is it transference from one to another? Yes, it is a mystery that allows gifts to reach others. The One who imparts also works jointly with the Giver of gifts. Interestingly, impartation produces a similarity between the giver and the recipient. How can we impart gifts or virtue to others? Through books, preaching, teachings, prophecies, God's Word, the laying on of hands, and even anointed cloths or clothing. We receive an impartation when we capture the spirit of the mantle that rests upon a man or woman of God, which could take place by association. In our church, every House of Peace leader, mentor, deacon, elder, and minister flows in the same anointing of miracles I do because I have imparted into each of their lives of the mantle that God has placed upon me.

Here are a few testimonies of some creative miracles we have seen in our ministry because of my having imparted my mantle to others:

In the middle of a service at our church, God glorified Himself by causing hair to grow on the head of a bald man. Three weeks prior to that day, I had declared that on that night the Lord would perform creative miracles and that even baldness would disappear by hair growing on heads. That night, as I began to pray, I included everyone who was bald and in need of hair. It was at that moment that hair began to grow on this gentleman, who had been bald for twenty years. This miracle was witnessed by everyone around him. When he realized what was happening, he ran to the altar to testify, carrying his driver's license, on which his photo attested to his prior baldness. He showed us how his hair had grown supernaturally. God did a creative miracle!

That same night, we had a similar testimony. For fifteen years, a man had suffered from high blood pressure. Four years prior, he had lost all the hair around the crown of his head. When he testified, he declared that while I prayed, rebuking all spirits of sickness, his head began to itch intensely, and when he went to scratch it, he felt hair where there had been none before. Needless to say, this man is now a very happy and grateful son of God because he enjoys normal blood pressure and has a full head of hair. Praise God!

The Purpose of the Anointing

Jesus taught His disciples about the kingdom in order to help them understand the purpose of power. The same is true with the anointing. We must know what the anointing is in order to use it. Otherwise, it will be worthless to us.

> The Spirit of the Lord is upon me, **for** he has anointed me to bring Good News to the poor. He has sent me to proclaim that captives will be released, that the blind will see, that the oppressed will be set free.
>
> (Luke 4:18 NLT, emphasis added)

The key word in this verse is *"for."* Why did the Holy Spirit descend upon Jesus? Note that each purpose listed is neither selfish nor personally beneficial but rather to bless others. We cannot forget that the anointing is given to heal the sick, to cast out demons, to preach the gospel, to perform miracles, and, most important, to exalt Jesus. This is the reason we were separated and consecrated for the ministry. When men and women use their anointing to self-proclaim, self-promote, or gain dishonest earnings to satisfy a personal need for fame and possessions, their end will be painful. There is a sick world out there, full of insecurities, fear, depression, sadness, bitterness, and loneliness. It is a world tormented by wicked spirits; empty, aimless, and in need of someone who is anointed to break strongholds, someone whom God can use to deliver it and give it hope.

> It shall come to pass in that day that his burden will be taken away from your shoulder, and his yoke from your neck, and the yoke will be destroyed because of the anointing oil.
>
> (Isaiah 10:27)

By His anointing, God wants to use your life by this anointing to break the yoke of slavery, addictions, drugs, alcoholism, and other vices.

In our ministry, each minister, elder, deacon, mentor, and House of Peace leader has been trained and has received an impartation of the anointing for healing and miracles that is upon my life. The proof of this lies in the countless miracles that God performs in the Houses of Peace and discipleships through our leaders. Let me share one of those testimonies:

During a monthly meeting of our personal discipleship ministry, Pastor Alberto Fonseca prayed over one of his disciples who was suffering from urinary incontinency, which caused her to urinate without realizing it. For this reason, she had to wear disposable diapers. The problem originated at birth. She had suffered from spina bifida, a congenital cleft of the spinal cord. She had surgery to correct her spine, but, in the process, her bladder was damaged. Her doctors determined that her bladder condition had no cure and that she would have to use diapers for the rest of her life. According to her testimony, when Pastor Fonseca prayed for her, she felt nothing except for a small, tickly sensation that traveled down to her womb. Then, for the first time in twenty-five years, this woman felt the need to urinate. During the days that followed, when she removed her diaper, it remained dry. It was then that she realized she had been healed. Years of shame, sadness, and depression were over. God had completely healed her!

In my many years of ministry experience, I have observed two different types of anointing, or mantles, operating over certain individuals on earth:

- **Generational mantles**

Generational mantles are transferred from natural, or spiritual, fathers and mothers to their sons and daughters. Whenever a mentor/disciple relationship is established, in time, the mantle is transferred from one generation to another, as from Moses to Joshua and from Elijah to Elisha.

• **Special mantles**

These mantles are given by God and placed directly upon certain men and women to carry out a specific mandate for a particular generation. Once the purpose is carried out, the mantle cannot be duplicated. We see an example of this in David, whom God called a man after His own heart. (See 1 Samuel 13:14.) Except for Jesus, we cannot find another man like David in the Bible. Even though he was a dysfunctional king, he received a special mantle for praise, worship, and warfare.

When we are given a special mantle, God will often give us a preview of what to expect in the ministry, as long as we persevere and remain faithful until the end. More than fifteen years ago, God told me what would happen in my ministry. He spoke to me first during a service I was preaching in Cuba. I saw all the sick receive healing instantly. Then, in Argentina, the Lord showed me the most powerful creative miracles I had ever seen up to that point. After that day, I did not witness miracles to such a degree until 2000. During those times, God was giving me a preview of what He was going to do through me. This was to encourage me to seek them. Today, I flow in that special anointing and witness God's glory manifesting everywhere I preach.

A special anointing will often be accompanied by a small preview of what will come in the future.

When something extraordinary takes place in our lives once or twice, it could be a preview of what is to come. Anointings are being loosened on the earth right now, including some that have never been seen before. Keep your eyes open. How many have abandoned their mantles? How many never accepted them? How many mantles—for music and teaching, for the apostle and prophet, for politics, worship, and spiritual warfare—are waiting for God's people to take them? How many anointed men and women with powerful mantles are on earth right now but do not have spiritual children who serve that mantle in preparation to inherit it later?

With these questions in mind, now is a good time to clarify that we will never wear a new mantle until we let go of the old capes of religion and tradition. If we are not ready to get rid of the old, we will not be ready to receive the new mantle.

> *And David said to Saul, "I cannot walk with these, for I have not tested them." So David took them off.*
> (1 Samuel 17:39)

Saul placed his armor on David before he faced Goliath, but it did not work because it was too heavy, making it impossible for David to move under its weight. Saul's armor symbolized the old, the traditional, and the religious—the old that many of us are used to wearing. Unlike David, who immediately removed the armor, we walk with religion and self-effort, even if we hate it and find it unproductive.

Sometimes, God allows us to experience a season of feeling burned-out, a season in which nothing happens, in order to help us remove the old mantle and receive a new one. In these cases, we may perceive in our spirits that there is something more, but we have no idea how to receive it. Other times, it causes frustration, desperation, or dissatisfaction to make us seek His face and thereby allow Him to give us the new mantle. This will not be an easy task because God has not called us to do anything easy. Therefore, we must be prepared to pay the price.

What Are the Consequences of Judging or Refusing a Mantle?

The Word teaches that we will receive a mantle the same way we receive a gift. If we do not respect it—if we criticize it, judge it, or reject it—we will not receive it.

> *He who receives a prophet in the name of a prophet shall receive a prophet's reward.* (Matthew 10:41)

The moment someone speaks badly about the mantle or anointing of a man of God, he schedules the funeral for his own mantle. The person who betrays a prophetic mantle will never again flow in the prophetic mantle. Likewise, the person who betrays the apostolic mantle will never again flow in the apostolic anointing.

What happened to the apostle Paul? He lived in Corinth for three and a half years. He taught, imparted, and gave his life for the people. Sadly, the people did not grow or mature. They remained as spiritual children. This happened because they did not receive the mantle that God had placed on Paul. However, the same apostle visited the Thessalonians for three weeks, was welcomed there as a man of God, and delivered a message that was accepted as God's Word. As a result, the Thessalonians grew, matured, and evangelized Macedonia.

How many mantles have been rejected by the church? I believe this is a major reason why the body of Christ is incomplete. We cannot live with only one measure, gift, or mantle. We need mantles for healing, miracles, prosperity, worship, wealth, knowledge, politics, government, and so forth. If we did not, God would not have provided these mantles.

What Has Happened to the Fivefold Ministries?

And [Jesus] *Himself gave some to be apostles, some prophets, some evangelists, and some pastors and teachers.*
(Ephesians 4:11)

This verse refers to what is commonly called the "fivefold ministry," which should still be active within the church today. Unfortunately, many churches fail to acknowledge and support all five roles, or mantles, within the church. When we reject the pastoral ministry, we fail to care for the sheep, and they are likely to lose their way. If we reject the teacher's mantle, we may perish for lack of knowledge. (See Hosea 4:6.) When we reject the evangelistic mantle, many souls are not saved. When we reject the ministry of the prophet, the church lacks important vision and direction concerning the things that God is doing and saying. If we reject the apostolic mantle, the church operates largely without direction, vision, edification, impartation, revelation, advancement of the kingdom, and supernatural power to perform miracles.

Every time we reject one of the fivefold ministries, the church suffers because God's power cannot manifest fully. When we receive a mantle, we don't necessarily fulfill that role. However, we do become active participants in the anointing that mantle radiates. Even if we are not apostles ourselves, when we welcome an apostle, the apostolic anointing flows through us. Some people reject certain mantles because they have seen others take them to the extreme with negative results. We cannot allow the past sins and errors of some to cause us to reject a God-given mantle, for He will give us the wisdom and discernment to use it properly.

Some mantles have never been used because they were rejected. The mantle you reject becomes the one that will judge you.

In traveling to other nations, I have noticed that wherever I and my anointing are welcomed, the people receive my mantle of miracles, supernatural power, signs, deliverance, evangelism, teaching, governmental anointing, and revelation of the Word. The anointing manifests fully in that place. However, in places where my mantle is not fully accepted, the people experience God's supernatural power only in the areas in which it is received.

For example, when I traveled to Venezuela, the people received me as God's apostle and my message as God's Word. Consequently, God did great things through me: healing, miracles, and extraordinary signs and wonders. The deaf, mute, and blind were healed, the lame were raised from their wheelchairs, and many who had been suffering from terminal illnesses were instantly healed and delivered.

Do not touch My anointed ones, and do My prophets no harm.
(1 Chronicles 16:22)

In this verse, the word *"touch"* has a negative connotation. It implies criticism, obstacles, or harm. This indicates that if anybody "touches" the anointed of God, they are, in fact, "touching" God. You cannot touch the anointed without touching the divine mantle that rests upon his or her life.

Consequences of Touching the Mantle

- **Aaron and Miriam touched Moses' mantle.**

Then Miriam and Aaron spoke against Moses because of the Ethiopian woman whom he had married.
(Numbers 12:1)

- **Judgment came upon Miriam.**

"Why then were you not afraid to speak against My servant Moses?"...Suddenly Miriam became leprous, as white as snow.
(Numbers 12:8, 10)

- **Judgment came upon Aaron.**

Take Aaron and Eleazar his son, and bring them up to Mount Hor; and strip Aaron of his garments and put them on Eleazar his son.
(Numbers 20:25–26)

Let me illustrate this point with the following testimony.

One day, a woman left the church because she was upset with me and our leadership. Not satisfied with merely leaving, she also went to the media and spoke harshly of me. She even joined with other pastors to criticize and judge my ministry. A short time later, I was informed that she had suddenly developed cancer. I prayed for her but felt in my heart that the reason such a terrible illness had befallen her was because she had dared to touch the mantle of God that is on my life. Without hesitation, I sent her a message informing her that I wanted to speak with her so her heart could heal, but she refused to come. Unfortunately, she died of cancer two years later.

As I write this, the Lord is speaking to my heart the hope that the truths expressed in this chapter will save many lives from spiritual, financial, relational, and physical death because many have been mistreating the mantle of God's anointed, not knowing how delicate this subject is. If these people do not repent, judgment will come upon their lives. But if they repent, God will restore them, and they will receive the benefits of the mantles.

The Main Enemy of the Anointing

The main enemy of the anointing is familiarity, which may cause us to take lightly, or to disrespect, the mantle upon a man or woman of God. This goes hand in hand with the familiarity people develop toward God's servants and their anointing. People who take their pastors' mantles lightly no longer receive or take notes when they preach or teach. They neither hear God's Word with reverence nor intend to obey it. They give priority to other things, and being under their mantles no longer gives them joy because they no longer expect to receive as before.

When someone becomes too familiar with the man or woman of God, he will not be able to gain anything from that person's mantle.

Placing a Demand on the Anointing, or Mantle

To place a demand on a God-given anointing, or mantle, is to express a deep desire or hunger for a supernatural manifestation of God's power. Demand manifests by faith. For example, when a pastor is preaching and he suddenly stops to call someone with a specific condition to come forward for prayer, deliverance, or healing, it is because a demand had been made. Some preachers struggle to minister and teach because of familiarity and conformity. When people conform, they no longer exert the same level of demand upon the anointing of a man or woman of God. As a result, the power of God fails to manifest within them. Familiarity produces conformity and disrespect, with the result being that people become unable to receive from that mantle. Many people around me, close to the anointing for miracles, healing, and deliverance, prefer to visit their doctors instead of giving me the opportunity to pray for them. I fully acknowledge that God uses doctors and medicine to heal, and that it is proper, and often necessary, to consult them. Without doing so, many people alive today would have died. As believers, however, we must go to God first. Unfortunately, many have become so familiar with their spiritual leaders that they no longer have faith in the power that flows from their mantles. At other times, it is out of shame or fear that they do not seek the man or woman of God, which also equals familiarity.

If a person cannot receive from my mantle, it means that he is not ready to receive it.

How Do Faith and the Anointing Work Together?

The anointing is never received by skeptics, only by people who exercise their faith. This is why, while preaching, one tends to reach out to one segment of the congregation more than the other. It is likely that someone in that sector is placing a demand on the anointing—that is, someone is exercising faith. People absorb the gift in the mantle, and, in the end, the preacher does not need to minister individually to these people, as they have already received through the Word.

When a person does not place a demand on the anointing, he or she stops being a recipient of the anointing.

Faith can keep a man preaching even when he does not want to continue. This is not always understood, but it is caused by someone placing a demand and not letting go until something happens.

Individual faith can powerfully influence the anointing on a man or woman of God.

How Do We Receive the Benefits of a Mantle?

I have asked the Lord what needs to be done for my anointing to flow through my spiritual children. Then, I noticed that some were already flowing in the fullness of my mantle, some had only a portion of it, and others barely had it. It was then that the Lord taught me four principles about receiving the benefits of the mantle, or the anointing:

> It is like the precious oil upon the head, running down on the beard, the beard of Aaron, running down on the edge of his garments. (Psalm 133:2)

1. Recognize the mantle.

To recognize the mantle is to realize that the leader is the person God has chosen as a teacher over our lives. This is the person who will take us to our inheritance—the one whom we must learn from and follow. That man or woman is the vessel

God will use to pour the anointing into our lives and loosen our purposes and destinies. He or she will also lead us to flow in the same level of his or her anointing.

2. Receive the mantle.

We must welcome this person as the anointed one of God and understand that his or her message is from the living Word of God. It is also important to understand that anointed men and women have weaknesses as well as strengths. Therefore, we cannot expect that person to be perfect *before* welcoming him or her.

You cannot receive the strengths of the anointed if you do not accept their weaknesses.

---

3. Honor the mantle.

Honor is demonstrated verbally and materially through obedience and submission. In the Old Testament, no one could approach a man of God with empty hands, not because the anointing could be purchased but because it was a matter of honor. The Bible demonstrates the power of honor when God affirms that if we give a glass of water to a prophet, we will have the prophet's reward. (See Matthew 10:41–42.)

Honor gives us access to the reward system of a man or woman of God.

This is the case of my spiritual son, Pastor Alejandro Espinoza from Honduras, whom God placed under my spiritual covering when his congregation numbered only about one hundred fifty people. Today, his congregation has increased to more than two thousand people, and God is using him to manifest supernatural healing, signs, miracles, and marvels. His church is one of the fastest growing in that Central American country.

4. Serve the mantle.

Serving the mantle implies working and sowing into the mantle without a personal agenda. It means loving the man of God and the mantle that God has deposited upon him. The Lord once said to me, "When your disciples and spiritual children obey these principles, they will flow under your same anointing." This has come to pass. I have witnessed it over and over again. Everyone who obeys these four principles will manifest the same anointing of the mantle that is upon me.

A good example of this can be seen in another of my spiritual sons, Pastor Miguel Bogaert from the Dominican Republic. He came under my spiritual covering when his ministry had only forty attendees. Five years later, his church had over four thousand active members, and God is powerfully using him to perform signs, miracles, and wonders in order to impact the Caribbean island where he lives.

*You are able only to carry the mantle
of the one you serve.*

What Signs Indicate that God Has Loosened a New Mantle?

- God gives hunger and thirst that cannot be satiated until receiving what is desired, and those who experience them place a demand on the mantle. If God were to cut off the flow of the anointing, I would end up doing courtesy prayers. Often, when I pass by people, I feel no hunger or thirst pulling on the anointing.

- God changes our spiritual appetites. If we used to settle for crumbs, now we want to eat better. We no longer want the spiritual milk of the Word, but we seek to satisfy our hunger with meat and vegetables. We no longer enjoy only inspirational and motivational messages because we want messages that help us grow, mature, and become disciplined so that we can commit to God's service and seek more of Him.

• God gives us a strong desire to change. Regardless of age, if you are ready for change, God will give you a new mantle and impartation. Some people want new wine before they are ready to change their wineskins; if that is the case, God will not be able to pour out His new wine upon them.

How Are the Mantle and Impartation Given?

• **God loosens the mantle directly upon the person.**

In most cases, the person receives a revelation—a mandate from God or a supernatural visitation—as it happened to Jesus and others.

• **A person transfers his or her mantle to another.**

This can happen in three ways: by atmosphere, by association, or by influence.

Your blessings and destiny are closely related with those to whom God has connected you.

This is the reason divine relationships are heavily attacked by the devil. The enemy does not fight in vain. When God connects us to someone, Satan will do anything he can to destroy that relationship because he knows that if we never make such a connection, our purpose will never be carried out and completed.

God will connect us to other people. Therefore, we must become wise discerners of relationships. Most of my disciples end up becoming my spiritual children. In that type of relationship, they capture the spirit of the mantle that is upon me and learn how the Holy Spirit flows through me. When they obey the four principles previously mentioned (recognize, receive, honor, and serve), they begin to flow with the same anointing. However, those who disconnect themselves from my spiritual covering without God's leading often lose their anointing because they have been cut off from my atmosphere, association, and influence.

The anointing you receive by association can be lost if you begin to criticize or dishonor the mantle you have received.

What Must Happen for God to Give Us a Mantle?

1. We must hunger for, thirst for, and desire it.

Those who genuinely desire the anointing are the best candidates for receiving it. In the natural, if we feel the hunger for it, we will tend to forget the norms of courtesy because we seek only to satisfy our yearnings. The same happens in the spirit realm. Only those who hunger and thirst for the anointing are candidates to receive a mantle and the anointing.

Hunger and thirst can manifest in an individual when he is fully aware of his personal need to receive the anointing.

Without this awareness, he will not seek the anointing with passion or risk anything to acquire it. However, in some instances, as time passes, that passion for the anointing begins to subside, and we stop being aware of the need for it in our lives. This is not the way it should be. I was once asked what I had to do to upkeep my yearning and hunger for God's power.

My answer was plain and simple: I am always fully aware of my need for God.

2. We must be prepared to pay the price.

The belief that the anointing is free is a great misconception.

How could I give something that has taken me twenty years to build to someone who is not willing to pay the price? If we are not willing to sacrifice, we are not willing to be persecuted for the sake of the mantle. Countless preachers have cheapened the anointing. Consequently, today's youth regard the pastoral office as one more career choice instead of a holy ministerial calling. This is one reason I don't lay hands on people hastily. I lay hands only upon those who are genuine in their hunger and thirst for God's supernatural power.

Why Lay Hands on Someone When Transferring a Mantle?

- To activate
- To impart
- To identify

I cannot activate something in you if you are not willing to do God's will. I cannot impart the anointing over you if you do not resolve to use it to bless others. Likewise, I will not lay hands on you if you do not identify with the anointing that is on me. How much do you desire the mantle that rests upon the man of God? How much do you love that man? Are you strong enough to endure the persecution the mantle will cause? Are you willing to accept criticism, persecution, and rejection? We are activating too many people who are rebellious by nature. Therefore, it is important for the pastor to carefully choose a leadership team he can activate with his mantle and impartation.

3. The anointing, or mantle, must be planted and not thrown away.

Fatherhood and discipleship are sown by continually teaching, training, and equipping the people. If a seed is simply thrown to the ground, it is wasted, but if it is planted, it grows and bears fruit. When the mantle, or the anointing, is planted, or sown, people begin to flow in the same mantle because that is what they received. Remember that every seed grows according to its species. I have used this principle to raise up hundreds of men and women around the world—apostles, prophets, pastors, evangelists, teachers, leaders, businesspeople, politicians, intercessors, elders, disciples, and mentors. All of them flow with the same anointing that I have. As the mentor/disciple or father/son relationship grows, the flow of the mantle and its manifestation also grows. This indicates that the mantle also is growing.

We will flow in the same anointing as the mantle we serve.

---

4. The mantle must be cultivated.

For the anointing to increase, we must cultivate our mantle. This will keep us permanently connected to the source of the mantle. If we fail to do this, the anointing will weaken. In my experience with my spiritual children sent to establish their own ministries, I have found that for those who disconnected themselves from my mantle, for whatever reason, the growth of their churches and the flow of God's power in their lives slowed down. In other words, they decelerated, and the anointing decreased. This happens when someone operates under an anointing that was received only by association. When people stop feeding their anointing through a relationship with the headship, the anointing is eventually lost.

5. We must develop covenantal relationships.

God will cause our relationships to change because one key to becoming carriers of the anointing is not to be emotionally tied to people who are potential obstacles to our receiving and flowing in a new anointing, especially if those people have a traditional, denominational, and rigid mentality that keeps them from changing for the better.

In conclusion, it is important to discern the present move of God. There are waves and moves of the Holy Spirit we cannot afford to overlook, or we will be left behind, only to realize later that God is no longer where we expect to find Him.

The church needs to constantly seek divine revelation. Its survival will be determined by the degree of preparation it undertakes in order to walk in the supernatural. God is raising a new generation of people who know how to walk in the dimension of eternity and know how to draw forth the wealth of the spiritual world. This generation will also acknowledge that the purpose of the anointing is to bless others by healing the sick and by performing miracles, signs, and wonders, as Jesus commanded. We were chosen and anointed for action. Now, we must take action because the power of God is already in us and upon us.

Summary

- The anointing, as an integral part of God's supernatural power, is the divine ability given to the believer to do the work of the ministry.

- The elements used to create the holy anointing oil were myrrh—symbolizing the suffering and price of the anointing; cinnamon—representing strength and stability of character required to flow in it; cane—representing the gifts and authority; cassia—signifying prayer, praise, and worship; and oil, which symbolizes the presence of the Holy Spirit as the One who anoints.

- The anointing is used to consecrate, identify, and prepare a man or woman to manifest God's glory.

- Gifts and talents without the anointing will never bring glory to God.

- There are two types of anointing: personal and corporate.

- Jesus had two mantles: the mantel of His deity, which is His glory; and the mantle of His humanity, which is His anointing. He took off His mantle of glory to carry out His ministry in His humanity.

- The mantle of the anointing is our spiritual covering, and we give portions of it to others through impartation.

- The anointing is used to bless others, not for personal or selfish motives.

- Generational and special mantles can be transferred, and each has a specific purpose.

- The greatest enemy of the anointing is familiarity with a man or woman of God or with the mantle of the anointing that is upon him or her.

- The anointing is activated by faith that demands action.

- To receive the benefits of a mantle, we must recognize it, honor it, and serve it.

- For God to give us a new mantle, we must have an insatiable hunger and thirst for the anointing and a clear change in spiritual appetite coupled with the strong desire to change.

- There are two ways or methods to transfer a mantle: God will loosen the mantle directly over an individual, or one will transfer his or her mantle to another through his or her influence.

- The steps to receiving a mantle and impartation are (1) a yearning for the anointing, (2) being prepared to pay the price, (3) sowing the mantle (rather than throwing it away), and (4) changing relationships.

7

Glory: The Third Dimension of the Supernatural

Chapters five and six covered the first two dimensions of the supernatural: faith and anointing. Now, let us enter into the third dimension, which is the glory of God. These three dimensions are different, yet they complement each other. In this chapter, you will learn how God's glory operates and how we can manifest it on earth through revealed knowledge. I have written this chapter to aid you in the transition from the anointing into God's glory and to awaken this present generation to the benefits of moving into, and permanently remaining within, the presence of God. Unfortunately, I know of very few men and women who are walking in the revelation and manifestation of the glory of God.

Glory, in the Beginning

And the LORD God formed man of the dust of the ground, and breathed into his nostrils the breath of life; and man became a living being. (Genesis 2:7)

In the beginning, God created man in His image and likeness, shaping him from the dust of the earth and breathing into him the breath of life. That breath included God's glory. At that moment, God imparted the fullness of His virtues, nature, and glory to man. In that realm, the mind of man functioned at 100 percent because the mind of the Spirit was in him to exercise dominion and lordship over creation. Within God's glory, mankind had no understanding of sickness, death, poverty, depression, or sadness because his original design did not recognize these trials. He did not have to wait to gather the harvest because waiting implies a space in time, and glory is eternity where everything is now. Plants and trees grew as each seed hit the ground. The Word teaches that when creation took place, everything was already fruitful and mature. Even Adam was spared the stages of growth that we must endure. It is important to stop here for a moment and note that Jesus did experience each stage of growth, and this is why He has the ability to comprehend what it feels like to be a child, a teenager, and an adult. He understands what it feels like to be rejected, judged, and condemned. But these experiences were unknown to Adam before the fall. In the dimension of glory, earth was completely fertile. Its order was harvest/seed rather than seed/harvest. Adam was so intelligent that he was able to name all the animals and exercise lordship over all created things without a problem. He was fully capable of carrying out this task effortlessly because he dwelled in the glory of God.

> *For all have sinned and fall short of the glory of God.*
> (Romans 3:23)

What happened after Adam sinned? I believe that when God went looking for Adam and Eve in the garden and talked with them, instead of spending much time with them, He cursed the earth and withdrew His presence. In fact, I believe that He then inhaled His glory from Adam's body. At that moment, man exited the dimension of glory and began to experience death, though not immediately. As an added note of interest, we could say that the residue of glory that lingered in Adam was enough for him to live to the age of nine hundred thirty years. That inheritance was passed down to several generations, and they also enjoyed years of life into the hundreds.

Everything that has God's glory has life. Death indicates an absence of His glory.

When Adam sinned, something shifted in the mind of man. Many lines of genuine knowledge were disconnected from their original source, and the human brain lost a major percentage of usage. Today, scientists have discovered that we use only a small percentage of our cerebral capacity, which could lead to the conclusion that Adam substituted limited rational knowledge for infinite revealed knowledge. In the case of Albert Einstein, whose ability to reason well exceeded that of the average human, he used a little more brain capacity than an average man. If the average man, despite his limitations, has been able to make so many discoveries, travel into space, and develop cures to countless sicknesses, among other achievements, imagine how spectacular Adam's mind must have been under God's glory. This is why we must recover our mental capacity. It is also what the Bible refers to when it urges us to renew our minds.

After Adam's fall, God cursed the land, and man was disconnected from His glory. Thus, again, the process of provision is no longer harvest/seed, as it was in the beginning, but seed/time/harvest.

> *While the earth remains, seedtime and harvest, cold and heat, winter and summer, and day and night shall not cease.*   (Genesis 8:22)

Today, we go from process to process, each process taking time to complete. As a result of the curse, which has left us dependent on time, we must wait to gather the harvest or reach a goal. This is precisely why God gave us faith—to break the law of time. When His presence manifests itself, everything in the natural accelerates, and the supernatural appears.

> *"Behold, the days are coming," says the LORD, "when the plowman shall overtake the reaper, and the treader of grapes him who sows seed."*   (Amos 9:13)

The key word in this verse is *"overtake."* God promises to loosen the house, the job, or anything else we need, as long as we believe we will receive it. I have seen God cancel debt instantaneously. This is one good reason for us to stay full of faith. Our seed will activate the promise of God to accelerate His provision.

Now that we understand what happened after Adam sinned, let's understand the revelation of glory.

What Is the Glory of God?

The Hebrew for "glory" is *kabowd*, which means "glory, honor, glorious, abundance." It comes from a root word meaning "to be heavy, be weighty...rich." *Kabowd* is used in describing wealthy men of great reputation, but it is also used to refer to God. In Greek, the word used for "glory" is *doxa*, meaning "splendor, brightness...magnificence, excellence, preeminence, dignity, grace." In essence, this word gives us the fundamental meaning of who God is—His attributes, virtues, character, nature, and perfection. God's glory is the intrinsic essence of His presence.

As we discuss the glory of God, it is also important to note that there exists the glory of men and the glory of the world. The Bible describes these types of glory as vain and temporal, consisting only of prestige, fame, position, comfort, reputation, and recognition.

> *The lust of the flesh, the lust of the eyes, and the pride of life; is not of the Father but is of the world.*   (1 John 2:16)

The Word also mentions the glory of terrestrial and celestial bodies. It teaches that the external glory reflected by a body shows the internal condition of the same. This external glory is the intrinsic value and worth of the body.

> *There are also celestial bodies and terrestrial bodies; but the glory of the celestial is one, and the glory of the terrestrial is another.*   (1 Corinthians 15:40)

God's glory is the visible and tangible manifestation of the fullness of His presence impacting the physical senses. It is God making Himself tangible. In the Old Testament, God manifested in the form of a cloud known as *shekinah*, which means "dwelling, settling." It refers to the dwelling or settling presence of God among His people, as well as the eminent, transcending presence of God. God manifests Himself in the physical realm. In other words, He goes from the spiritual realm into the natural realm. *Shekinah* comes from the root word *shakan*, "to settle down, abide, dwell, tabernacle, reside." God's will and desire have always included dwelling, resting, and living among His people.

God's glory is the manifested presence of Jehovah.

- **God appeared to Abraham.**

The God of glory appeared to our father Abraham when he was in Mesopotamia, before he dwelt in Haran.

(Acts 7:2)

The physical manifestation of God's glory transformed Abraham forever, changing his life, motives, priorities, and intentions and prompting him to seek the Promised Land. Likewise, anyone who experiences a visitation of God's glory should be transformed forever. People transformed by God's glory receive a revelation from God and bring the glory into the natural dimension.

- **God manifested His glory to the Israelite nation.**

So it was always: the cloud covered it by day, and the appearance of fire by night. (Numbers 9:16)

God manifested His glory to the Israelites in the form of a pillar of cloud and a pillar of fire. The cloud protected the people from the sweltering heat of the desert during the day, and the fire kept them warm at night, when the temperatures dipped to near freezing. Under the protective covering of that glory—

shekinah—many supernatural events took place: the Red Sea opened before them, manna descended from heaven, and their footwear never wore out. During the forty years they walked the desert, no one experienced sickness, and God provided water from a rock and kept the giants from destroying them. These are only a few of the supernatural events that took place. God's glory also manifested in the shape of a cloud when Solomon's temple was dedicated. It was the sign that informed the people that Jehovah was dwelling among them.

- **God revealed His glory through Christ.**

  And the Word became flesh and dwelt among us, and we beheld His glory, the glory as of the only begotten of the Father, full of grace and truth. (John 1:14)

  Jesus came to reveal the Father's glory—the glory that was lost by Adam. Through His death and resurrection, Jesus led us back to that dimension of glory where we could walk once more as Adam did in the beginning.

  But we see Jesus, who was made a little lower than the angels, for the suffering of death crowned with glory and honor, that He, by the grace of God, might taste death for everyone. For it was fitting for Him, for whom are all things and by whom are all things, in bringing many sons to glory.... (Hebrews 2:9–10)

Jesus endured our shame so we could share in His glory.

Everything the Father is—His virtues, attributes, character, nature, power, authority, and grace—was manifested in His Son. Furthermore, Jesus promised to manifest Himself to those who obeyed His Word.

Just before His arrest, Jesus prayed to the Father, asking Him to return the glory that mankind had lost so that each believer could live in its manifestation.

As You sent Me into the world, I also have sent them into the world. And for their sakes I sanctify Myself, that they also may be sanctified by the truth.…And the glory which You gave Me I have given them, that they may be one just as We are one:…that they may behold My glory which You have given Me. (John 17:18–19, 22, 24)

In the following testimony, you will be able to appreciate what happens when we walk in the dimension of God's glory:

A man infected with HIV visited our church. At the time, he was only a carrier of the virus, but, as the illness began to manifest itself, he started to feel weaker and weaker until even his skin color began to change. He became very pale and suffered from chronic fatigue. His condition caused him great stress. He was unable to sleep, frequently vomited, and had dark blotches on his skin that were spreading across his body. His condition worsened to the point that his immune system completely shut down. When he came to church, I prayed for him and declared his healing from the dimension of God's glory. I knew that his sickness was incurable according to human science, but I also knew of God's supernatural power, which is capable of doing the impossible. Because that man's desire to live was so great, he received the Word and demanded his healing. In the same slow and progressive way he had seen his illness advance, day by day, he also began to watch it disappear. The blotches started to fade, and lab tests confirmed that his immune system was showing signs of improvement. A short time later, he had regained his strength and vitality. Eventually, God healed him completely! Today, he is a minister in our church, a man with a powerful gift of service, a grateful heart for God, and a passion for the ministry of intercession.

How Do We Enter into the Manifestation of God's Glory?

Holy, holy, holy is the LORD of hosts; the whole earth is full of His glory! (Isaiah 6:3)

Scripture affirms that the earth is full of God's glory, but the channel—or tool—that grants access to the manifestation of glory in the natural realm is revelation, not reason. While it is true that God's presence is everywhere, it is also true that He does not manifest everywhere.

God created the heavens and the earth and filled them with His glory. However, I want to highlight Genesis 1, which informs us that before God initiated the process of creation, He sent His Holy Spirit to set up camp with His energy—His glory—in order to make creation possible.

> *And the Spirit of God was hovering over the face of the waters.* (Genesis 1:2)

When God plans to do something, He first sends His Holy Spirit, followed by His Word.

Paul made reference to God's energy, His glory, and affirmed the following:

> *To this end I also labor, striving according to His working [energeia] which works [energeo] in me mightily.*
> (Colossians 1:29)

The literal translation of this verse suggests that Paul worked hard and gave his best because of the energy, or power, God gave him. This energy activated a miraculous power within Paul that elevated his capacity, potential, and authority.

God's energy has been here since the beginning, but it manifests itself only through revealed knowledge. Let us look at an example of this.

Have you ever felt completely exhausted when you entered church but had your strength renewed and your hope encouraged when God's presence manifested? If the answer is yes, it is because you experienced a small touch of God's powerful energy.

God's glory provides the necessary energy to create any matter.

God's glory has been upon the earth since creation. Ever since the fall of man, however, we have been unable to see or work with it. But if His glory exists on the earth with the power of creation, then God can create a new heart, lung, ear, eye, arm, or any other organ that is missing. But this happens only when the Holy Spirit moves and God acts on His Word. The key, therefore, is knowing how to call forth a visible manifestation of God's glory in the natural realm.

God's glory makes no sense without revealed knowledge.

Miracles occur when we declare the Word of God from the dimension of His glory.

This is the story of a lady who was diagnosed with pulmonary tuberculosis at the age of nine. At that time, the doctors removed one of her lungs to stop any advancement of the illness. In the years that followed, although the illness was under control, her breathing capacity never returned to normal due to her missing lung. She felt better, but she did not feel well. For the next twenty years, she suffered from extreme exhaustion, chronic pain, and sporadic bleeding. As time when on, her lung began to bleed more frequently. Her doctors agreed that her symptoms were getting progressively worse.

The first time this woman visited our church, it was because someone invited her to attend one of our Healing and Miracle Services. During the service, when I declared that creative miracles would take place, she believed God and took hold of her miracle. Instantly, she felt herself breathing at a faster and stronger pace. This was an experience she was unfamiliar with. Then, she took a step of faith and ran to the altar. Afterward, she returned to her doctor, who ordered that X-rays be taken. When these new X-rays were compared to her previous ones, the doctors made a discovery. She now had two lungs. "This is a miracle!" exclaimed the surprised doctor. God had created a new, healthy, fully-functioning lung within her. "God gave me a new lung! I have two good lungs!" shouted this daughter of God.

> ### God's glory is on earth. Now, all we need is the knowledge to manifest it.

What Is Revealed Knowledge?

For the earth will be filled with the knowledge of the glory of the LORD, as the waters cover the sea.
(Habakkuk 2:14)

The word *"knowledge,"* as used in this verse, is the Hebrew word *yada*, meaning "to know, learn to know...to perceive and see, find out and discern...to discriminate, distinguish...to know, be acquainted with." It is also used in Genesis 4:1 to describe sexual intimacy between Adam and Eve.

In Greek, the two words for *"knowledge"* are *gnosis* or *epignosis*. The former is scientific or theoretic knowledge, and the latter refers to observable, practical knowledge. *Epignosis* means "precise and correct knowledge." Revealed knowledge, then, comes to our spirits when we have a close, intimate relationship with God. It is then revealed by the Holy Spirit. In this way, knowledge is something to be experienced, not stored.

> ### Knowledge will never become ours until we obey it, practice it, and experience it.

God's glory must be revealed by the Holy Spirit; it cannot be discovered by research or understood by reason. It must be experienced! His glory cannot be enclosed in a message because it can be initiated only by God and for God. Thus, there is a formula or pattern that can be followed in order to activate and flow in His glory. What is written in this chapter is simply what God revealed to me in order to establish a foundation for what is about to occur. I believe that our generation will see the former glory (the miracles of the Old Testament) and latter glory (the miracles Jesus predicted would occur in the church) manifesting together. God is raising apostles and prophets to bring this revelation to our generation. He is opening the heavens and pouring out the revelation we need to manifest His glory, because, without it, we will never see beyond what we can see today. For centuries, the church has been seeking manifestations of power without success, not because God has chosen not to manifest but because the church lacks the required faith and knowledge to manifest His glory. This will take place only when the necessary knowledge is revealed.

A revelation from God will undoubtedly lead you to a supernatural experience.

If ever there was a time for God to deliver the revealed knowledge of His glory, I believe it is now. Many prophets, including Isaiah, Habakkuk, and Haggai, prophesied of the glory but never fully experienced it. They died with their hopes rooted in this era, which leads us to deduce that we are living in the final move of God, in which the earth will be full of His knowledge and glory. Then, we will experience the greatest manifestations ever seen in history, and no man will be able to attribute that glory to himself.

For God's glory to manifest, it must be captured, received, and recognized by our spirits through the revelation of the Holy Spirit. I know several people who have experienced manifestations of

God's glory but were unable to continue in it because their knowledge was imparted by someone else. In other words, they lacked their direct revelation from God.

If a person never receives revelation, he will not see continuous manifestations.

The mistake many people make is that they move in the glory for a short time and later return to the anointing because they failed to allow God to take the initiative. Thus, they learned to operate by faith under the anointing, but they never learned to move in the glory because it is an unknown dimension in which the initiative belongs to God. Glory demands a greater degree of humility and dependence on God. It demands pure motives and boldness in the Holy Spirit.

God will not visit us with His glory beyond the revelation we have of it.

If the Lord visits us with His glory and we are not ready for it, it can kill us. If He brings forth unusual manifestations, creative miracles, signs, and wonders, but we lack the revelation to receive them, we will judge and criticize what is happening, thereby grieving the Holy Spirit. When the manifestation of God's glory comes, we must know how to deal with it. Otherwise, we will be like Uzzah, who disobeyed God, even with the best of intentions, by reaching out to steady the ark of the covenant when God had strictly forbidden that it be touched.

Then the anger of the LORD was aroused against Uzzah, and God struck him there for his error; and he died there by the ark of God. (2 Samuel 6:7)

The glory we preach can also kill us.

How Do Glory, Faith, and the Anointing Operate?

When reviewing the dimensions of the supernatural, we understand how they work together and how they differ. Faith is the ability given to the believer by God to have dominion over time, space, and matter. Anointing is the ability given to the believer by God to do whatever He has called him or her to do. It is Jesus working through humanity. Glory is the presence of God manifested in visible form. It is God doing His works and operating according to His sovereignty and initiative.

Now, let us see how faith, the anointing, and glory—the three dimensions of the supernatural—operate.

That you, being rooted and grounded in love, may be able to comprehend with all the saints what is the width and length and depth and height; to know the love of Christ which passes knowledge. (Ephesians 3:17–19)

For in [the gospel] *the righteousness of God is revealed from faith to faith.* (Romans 1:17)

As we established earlier, *"from faith to faith"* means we are able to go from one dimension of faith to another dimension of faith.

The apostle Paul, according to the original text written in Greek, affirmed the following:

But we all...are being transformed into the same image from glory to glory. (2 Corinthians 3:18)

There are many levels of the anointing. With spiritual gifts, we can minister to one or several members of the body of Christ. With the anointing, we can reach multitudes. With the glory, we can reach and impact nations. If something took ten years to accomplish under the anointing, we will be able to do it in one year under the glory.

This is what happened to Peter at the Sea of Tiberias. After he had spent a night of fishing without success, Jesus appeared on the shore and gave the order to cast the nets on the other side of the boat. It took the fishermen only a few minutes to fill the net with hundreds of fish. (See John 21:1–8.) When the glory of God manifests, everything accelerates.

The same thing can happen in churches that stopped growing after reaching a few hundred members. When the glory of God manifests, they supernaturally explode, growing into the thousands in a short time.

The Bible relates a similar event in Acts when the apostles started to preach the gospel of the kingdom. In one day, after the apostles received the power of the Holy Spirit, three thousand people were converted and baptized. (See Acts 2:41.)

The Manifested Glory—the Presence of God—Operates on the Basis Of:

• God's sovereignty

This means that God does what He wants, when He wants, and how He wants. We have grown accustomed to denying the Holy Spirit the freedom to exercise His divine sovereignty in our personal lives and in our churches. Because of this, the services we attend are monotonous and lack supernatural manifestations. We must allow the Holy Spirit to manifest the sovereignty of God and allow Him to do as He wills.

> *Do not be hasty to go from his presence. Do not take your stand for an evil thing, for he does whatever pleases him.* (Ecclesiastes 8:3)

• God's initiative

Jesus is the Head of the church. Therefore, He must initiate the action and move as He wants. However, there are times when God does not initiate the action because He has already told us in His Word what to do. When this happens, it is best to do what

He has commanded us to do, making sure that we understand His command and do not invent something just to get it over and done with. What I am saying is that we must do what God has ordained, such as evangelizing, making disciples, healing the sick, and casting out demons. Let us not confuse this with what King Saul did—he waited for the prophet Samuel to offer the sacrifice unto the Lord, but, since the prophet delayed, he decided to do it himself—which he was not permitted to do. (See 1 Samuel 13:6–14.) Do you see the difference?

Most believers understand the concept of God's sovereignty, but what they don't understand is how to live in it by faith.

- **Always waiting for God to take the initiative**

On occasions when God's presence has not yet manifested, we must then exercise our faith, anointing, and gifts. If we do nothing, *always* waiting for God to take the initiative, then we are working in the extreme. For example, if we feel that the Holy Spirit has not touched the lost, we should still, by faith, make the call for salvation. Since God has already commanded us to do this, we should not wait for Him to make the next move. Clearly, the next move is our responsibility.

- **Always taking the initiative from the human point of view**

As I explained before, this statement refers to churches that are conducted entirely by man-made plans, which lead only to doing works that are void of God's power and presence. This, of course, is another extreme.

What Is the Difference between Glory and Anointing?

- The anointing is for the earth and can operate only in our world. Glory testifies of the powers of the coming age because it is the atmosphere of heaven. Just as air is the atmosphere of earth, glory is the atmosphere of heaven.

- The anointing prepares us for the glory that is God's presence.

- The anointing gives us the ability or power to stand in His presence; the glory *is* His presence.

- With the anointing, the believer takes the initiative through his or her gifts and faith. With glory, God takes the initiative.

- In the anointing, faith places a demand on the mantle of an individual; in the glory, faith places a demand upon God's presence.

- The anointing was given to heal the sick, but the glory of God makes sickness illegal.

- In the anointing, Jesus is the Healer; in the glory, He is the Creator.

- We work in the anointing; we worship and rest in the glory.

- In the anointing, we experience God's power leaving us; in the glory, the power comes directly from God.

After operating under the anointing for a long time, I feel physically exhausted because people place a demand upon the anointing God put in me. This is similar to what Jesus must have felt when the bleeding woman touched His robe and received healing.

> *Jesus, immediately knowing in Himself that power had gone out of Him, turned around in the crowd and said, "Who touched My clothes?"* (Mark 5:30)

When I operate in the glory, however, instead of feeling tired, I feel full of energy because God is doing all the work. In the glory, God does not need my human effort. The anointing is the divine power God gives His servants to carry out His calling on earth. The anointing is amazing, incredible, and holy, and we will continue to operate under it whenever the glory or presence of God does not manifest.

Crossing Over from Anointing to Glory

God is leading many on the path of transition from the anointing into the glory so that they can enter into the river of God's *shekinah*. Those who resist the transition will become stuck and unable to participate in the final move of God's glory. For fear of excess demands, many have decided not to make the transition. But if God sees a sincere heart that is desperate for His glory, He will not allow the faithful to be deterred.

We, however, will not boast beyond measure, but within the limits of the sphere which God appointed us.
(2 Corinthians 10:13)

A man knows he is in the dimension of glory when he no longer operates in his personal measure of faith or anointing.

To pass from one level of anointing to another requires a strong set of spiritual exercises, which include fasting, prayer, and the thorough study of God's Word. However, after advancing through various levels of anointing, there will come a time in a person's life when he will reach a peak and can go no further. When this happens, the person is ready to make the transition from anointing to glory. The transition into glory, however, requires revealed knowledge, even though spiritual exercise will also be necessary.

The anointing will not grow unless we use it with discipline and good stewardship.

We must decide to make the transition from anointing to glory. If you have reached a level of faith in which nothing new is happening, you are a candidate to enter into the dimension of glory. I believe that God is raising a generation of pioneers who hunger and thirst for His glory and who are willing to enter into the next dimension of faith and a higher dimension of glory, men and women who are willing to pay the price and who wholeheartedly desire to see the manifestation of the glory of God.

> *O God, You are my God; early will I seek You; my soul thirsts for You; my flesh longs for You in a dry and thirsty land where there is no water. So I have looked for You in the sanctuary, to see Your power and Your glory.*
> (Psalm 63:1–2)

Until now, God's desires for this generation have not been satisfied. Now, only God's move will fill us completely. Cry out to God so the revelation of His glory will descend on your life in this season.

A Contrast between Darkness and Glory

Today, the people of the world are shrouded by darkness. The headlines are filled with wars, famines, earthquakes, hurricanes, tsunamis, violence, genocide, and pestilence. Cruelty and injustice permeate the news each day.

> *For behold, the darkness shall cover the earth, and deep darkness the people; but the LORD will arise over you, and His glory will be seen upon you.* (Isaiah 60:2)

As the darkness grows darker, His light shines brighter. We must choose sides; you are either with Jesus or against Him. Do you love the light? Then, run toward it. Do you love the darkness? If our works are evil, we will reject the light, which is His glory. Will you run to the light? Will you be part of the glory, or will you continue to live in darkness? Are you willing to pay the price to move in His glory? The life of the believer becomes brighter with each passing day, more glorious than the dawn.

> *He who is unjust, let him be unjust still; he who is filthy, let him be filthy still; he who is righteous, let him be righteous still; he who is holy, let him be holy still.*
> (Revelation 22:11)

Now is the time to choose. We cannot remain neutral. We must not be deceived into thinking that salvation is a static state, because it is not. Salvation is a way of life in which we are to go from one dimension of glory into another dimension of glory.

The essence of Christian living consists in becoming like Jesus, or likened to His image.

Jesus will come for a glorious church that will manifest God's tangible and visible glory with miracles, healings, signs, and wonders. Every believer who is sanctified and separated for Him will be a vessel of the latter and former glory that will invade this world. I believe the day is coming when a carrier of God's glory will enter a hospital, and all the patients within will be instantaneously healed as soon as that person steps through the door. I believe the day is coming when it will be a normal occurrence for believers to raise the dead. In these last days, I believe that the channels of communication will cover all types of manifestations performed by average Christians who choose to separate themselves for God's exclusive use. I consider myself to be one of these Christians because I have an insatiable desire to see the former and latter glory manifest. It will be unlike anything that has ever been seen. Dear reader, the decision is yours, and I sincerely pray that you will make the right one.

The earth is full of the glory of God, and He is revealing it to this generation in order to bring great manifestations. God is raising a generation with a different mentality—a generation of those who are willing to run and be carriers of His divine glory. We must decide today if we want to enter into the realm of His glory or not. This is not a matter of one man doing something but of something being initiated by the sovereignty of God that manifests miracles, signs, and wonders. It is a blessing to be alive and witness God's glory manifest everywhere, right in front of our eyes!

Summary

- Adam was born under the glory. He never experienced the process of growth or had to wait for the earth to produce fruit. Everything produced fruit instantaneously. He had a brilliant mind because it was the mind of the Spirit of God.

- The moment Adam sinned, God inhaled His glory from Adam's body, and man became a mortal being sustained by the residue of the glory he once enjoyed.

- God gave us faith to interrupt the process of time, accelerate the natural, and manifest the supernatural.

- The glory reflects the inner being. God's glory is the visible and tangible manifestation of the fullness of His presence.

- God revealed His glory through Jesus and all His divine virtues.

- The channel through which we can reach the glory of God is revealed knowledge.

- When God wants to do a miracle, He moves His Holy Spirit and speaks the Word—then, He is able and capable of creating anything.

- God will not visit us with His glory beyond the revelation we have of it.

- Faith and the anointing operate by human initiative; glory works by divine initiative.

- The glory operates on the basis of God's sovereignty and His initiative. To experience it, we must never go to the extreme and operate by human initiative but always waiting for divine initiative.

8

Miracles, Signs, Wonders, and Casting Out Demons

As we examine the Bible, we discover it to be a book full of miracles, signs, and wonders, from Genesis all the way to Revelation. It is an account of the most important events realized by a supernatural God. On more human terms, Jesus, the Son of God, whose existence appears throughout history, walked the earth, healing the sick and performing other miracles as clear signs of His deity. After His resurrection, the Son of God delegated His mission to His disciples by giving them the same supernatural power He had exhibited on earth. (See John 14:12.) But it did not end there. The mission and power He delegated extend to the believers of this generation so that we, too, can perform miracles, signs, and wonders in His name.

Jesus has not changed. He is the same yesterday, today, and forever. (See Hebrews 13:8.) His conception and birth through a young virgin was a miracle. His knowledge and wisdom, which confused the erudite experts in the law, were miracles. His entire ministry was a torrent of miracles that inspired awe and wonder in the multitudes that witnessed them. His crucifixion, death, and resurrection were also miraculous events. As its name implies, the book of Acts is filled with the many miracles, signs, and wonders performed by the disciples of Jesus. In almost every chapter, there are descriptions of supernatural "acts" that took place after the Holy Spirit descended upon the faithful. Through them, the early church was able to proclaim

His name with power and supernatural evidence. Today, we have the same privilege.

Jesus delegated His ministry of miracles to the church, which angered the Jewish leaders of His time and worried the Roman government. Today, we are the continuation of His miracle ministry. When miracles are absent from Christianity, there is nothing new to offer an unbelieving world other than another form of religion with the appearance of godliness.

Christianity is life—the nature of Jesus manifested through His people. In the Old Testament, the purpose of miracles was to divert people's attention from their worship of pagan gods and to lead them in worship of the only true God. In those days, when miracles ceased, people quickly reverted to their old rituals and pagan ceremonies. The same thing is happening today. Most churches are full of people who need a miracle from God today, because, tomorrow, they will look for it somewhere else.

My Experience with Jesus, the Miracle-Working God

I have enjoyed many incredible personal experiences with my beloved Jesus:

- I have seen Jesus perform miracles, signs, and wonders in His Word.

- I have personally witnessed the real, resurrected Christ performing miracles, signs, and wonders through men and women, both in the past and the present time.

- I have personally experienced, and continue to experience, being used by God to perform miracles, signs, and wonders.

- I work to teach, train, and equip others to be used by God in ministries of miracles.

I have witnessed the blind see, the deaf-mute hear and speak, and the lame walk. I have seen people suffering from cancer,

AIDS, and other supposedly incurable diseases walk away completely healed. I have seen flesh and bone created where there were none before. I have witnessed wonderfully unusual miracles, such as the growth of new teeth, the appearance of hair on bald heads, and the loss of weight in mere seconds. All of these miracles were done in the powerful name of Jesus. No longer must we go back to the days of the apostles to read of miracles. We can see them with our own eyes. Jesus was raised from the dead, He is alive, and He continues to perform miracles today. I have experienced these miracles in over forty countries, and you can experience them, too.

You can know that Jesus lives by seeing Him perform the same miracles He did while He walked on earth.

If the Christianity you practice is not based on the miraculous, then all you have is a dead religion. The world needs to *see* the resurrected Christ, the One who lives and continues to perform miracles as a sign of His love. One problem with religion today is its inability to bring Jesus into the present—into the now. People focus on the past and pray for the future, but they ignore the present. If Jesus is unable to do miracles today, why call Him God? If God cannot perform miracles, how can we refer to Him as being love? I pray that while you read this chapter, the extent of supernatural experiences I have witnessed and shared with you in this book will also take place in your life. I am praying for you to receive a creative miracle of healing and, later, to be able to go and do the same for others.

Genuine faith brings Jesus into the now.

I believe that God is loosening the most extraordinary miracles, signs, and wonders the world has ever seen. Each miracle will impact cities, nations, and continents, as happened in the book of Acts. This will cause people to kneel before Christ and believe that He is Lord.

In order to understand a few facts about the supernatural, let's define a few fundamental terms. Furthermore, let's examine the difference between them.

What Is Healing?

In the Greek text of the New Testament, several words are used to describe healing, although I will touch on only the three that are used most often. The first is *iasis*, which means "a healing, cure." It generally refers to an act of healing, such as:

> *Behold, I cast out demons and perform cures [iasis] today and tomorrow, and the third day I shall be perfected.*
> (Luke 13:32)

The second word, *therapeia*, means "a service rendered by one to another...a specific medical service: curing, healing," but it could refer to services other than healing. The word "therapy" derives from this word.

> *They followed Him; and He received them and spoke to them about the kingdom of God, and healed those who had need of healing [therapeia].* (Luke 9:11)

The third word, *iama*, is a much more complex term because, in addition to being defined as "a means of healing, remedy, medicine," it derives from a root word that also means "to make whole...to free from errors and sins, to bring about (one's) salvation." This was the ministry of Jesus, as seen in the following verse.

> *God anointed Jesus of Nazareth with the Holy Spirit and with power, who went about doing good and healing [iaomai] all who were oppressed by the devil, for God was with Him.* (Acts 10:38)

The following is a testimony of this kind of healing salvation in a person's life:

During a testimonial service, a lady came to the altar after being diagnosed with an autoimmune illness that was attacking and destroying several of her internal organs, including her liver. She was suffering from spontaneous bleeding, and her doctors had warned that she was at risk of dying. In addition, she also suffered from diabetes, and kidney dialysis was becoming a part of her daily routine. As part of her treatment, she had undergone approximately three hundred blood transfusions.

When we prayed for her in church, the Lord did an extraordinary healing. A few days after we prayed for her, she found that she was able to walk normally. In the days that followed, she began to recover progressively. Today, she testifies that she is born again and completely healed. Medical tests have confirmed her health status prior to her miracle—a condition that was without hope, medically. They further document the fact that, today, she is completely healthy. God's power healed her supernaturally. Today, she remembers the diagnosis that warned her that she would never recover. "But, I am alive," she confirms with a smile, "because God healed me!"

They will lay hands on the sick, and they will recover.
(Mark 16:18)

I know many believers who personally understand what Paul meant when he confessed that he had a thorn in his flesh. (See 2 Corinthians 12:7.) I know of those who have experienced Job's boils (see Job 2:7), Timothy's stomach pain (see 1 Timothy 5:23), and much more. Some think that sickness is a punishment sent by God, or that their suffering brings glory to God. Others use the Bible to try to justify their illnesses. None of these things is scripturally correct. Few of them can quote verses on healing because pastors have failed to teach on the subject.

My dear brothers and sisters, if we fail to teach and preach on the supernatural miracles of God, people will lack the faith to believe in miracles, and unbelievers will not be persuaded to trust in God.

According to Scripture, the power of sickness was destroyed by Christ over two thousand years ago. If this is so, why are people still getting sick? In truth, sickness expired the day Jesus paid the price for our iniquities on the cross of Calvary. Therefore, it is illegal for sickness to enter the bodies of believers. Healing is not a divine gift; it is a legal right. Yet the church continues to seek the "gift" of healing more than the "right" of healing.

Healing is a legal right that belongs to the believer, for his or her life, and to impart into the lives of others.

What Is a Miracle?

As I mentioned earlier, the Greek word for "miracle" is *dynamis*, which means "strength power, ability...inherent power, power residing in a thing by virtue of its nature." Miracles, therefore, manifest God's supernatural power. They are God's visible, spontaneous, and sudden intervention into the normal course of an individual's life, an interruption of the natural laws of time, space, and matter.

Truly the signs of an apostle were accomplished among you with all perseverance, in signs and wonders and mighty deeds. (2 Corinthians 12:12)

The following testimony shows the undeniable works of power that God performs:

While I was ministering in the Republic of El Salvador in Central America among some fifteen hundred Christian leaders, God's glory suddenly descended, and several people saw a visible cloud of His glory in the auditorium. When God's glory manifests, miracles begin to take place without any need for prayer. They take place not because of human anointing but because God chooses to perform miracles in His perfect will. Among those present was a doctor who, several years prior, had her auditory system removed and the opening of her ear completely closed. It was physiologically impossible for her to hear anything on that side of her head. Under the presence of the glory of God, however, she came to the altar, crying tears of joy to testify of God's great power. "I can hear on the side of my head on which the ear was removed, the side that doesn't have an auditory system!" No one was more qualified than she, a doctor, to testify and confirm this miracle. Medically and physically speaking, it was impossible for her to hear through that ear, but God had created a new auditory system. It happened in the midst of the presence of His glory. God is amazing!

What Is the Difference between a Healing and a Miracle?

A miracle is an instantaneous event that is evident to the human senses, while healing is progressive. So, a miracle produces a change that goes beyond healing. In the aforementioned testimonies, we note that in healing, God restored human organs to their proper function. But in the case of a miracle, God creates something that was not there before. Everyone wants miracles. Humanity is crying out for a living God. The call for a miracle is not a sign of ignorance or weakness but an intense desire to touch the invisible God and to see Him in action. Some maintain that education can take the place of miracles, and that, therefore, we don't need them any longer. Regardless of how effective education can be, it will never eliminate or nullify the need for the supernatural.

A miracle performed in the name of Jesus is more valuable than a year of academic theory.

This is a powerful testimony that demonstrates God's miraculous intervention:

During a service that we held in Mexico, a fifteen-year-old young man, accompanied by his mother, came forward to testify. He had arrived at the service in a wheelchair because of a condition that his doctors had diagnosed as chronic renal failure, a condition that destroys kidney function. In essence, they had told the young man that he was slowly dying. According to the doctors, his liver was too small and his heart was too large. As a result, his kidneys were seriously compromised, and his physical growth had stopped due to the illness.

When this young man came to the altar, he could not stop crying. I asked him why he was crying, and all he could say was, "I am crying because I am happy. I was going to die, but today, God healed me!" He and his mother had traveled from a small town two hours away, thanks to the help of friends who had prayed for God to perform a miracle. This young man was testifying to the world. He cried tears of joy, knowing that God had performed a powerful healing miracle in his life. He no longer needed to use his wheelchair. His heart was beating with a normal rhythm, and he had two newly created and fully functioning kidneys. When I asked his mother what she was feeling, she simply said, "The best Doctor healed my dying son." God had healed him!

What Is a Sign?

In the New Testament, *sign* comes from the Greek word *semeion*, which means "a sign, mark, token…miracles and wonders by which God authenticates the men sent by him." A sign is a demonstration of God's love or a seal that signifies that a person is distinguished or acknowledged. *Semeion* refers to a wondrous occurrence that takes place in an unusual way and transcends the common course of the natural world. God uses signs to authenticate those He sends, as well as to prove that the cause he or she is defending also comes from Him. The signs of God are used not only to help people but also to give glory to His Son, Jesus.

God performs signs as allegories to communicate a great truth of the kingdom and of Jesus.

On this point, we must pay close attention because there is a great difference between recognizing the signs that follow us and worshipping those signs. God prohibits our worship of signs. Yes, signs will follow those He sends, but only when their passion for God goes beyond their passion for the appearance of signs.

Here is an example of a sign we experienced while serving God in Mexico:

During a healing service, a man whose left thumb was shorter than his right thumb by almost an inch prayed with his eyes closed, asking God for a creative miracle for his thumb. At that moment, he felt the sensation of heat in his hand. As he opened his eyes, imagine his surprise to see that his left thumb had grown! He placed both of his hands together and showed those around him that both of his thumbs were now the same size. This man was deeply touched, crying over what God had done for him. Beyond the miracle, however, this also served as a sign to all those who were present that God was restoring the apostolic ministry in Mexico. The glory always belongs to God!

Now that we know the difference between a miracle, a healing, and a sign, let us look at the effects of signs, the meaning of wonders, and the casting out of demons.

What Seven Signs Prove the Deity of Jesus?

This beginning of signs Jesus did in Cana of Galilee, and manifested His glory; and His disciples believed in Him.

(John 2:11)

As I mentioned in a previous chapter, the gospel of John is structured around seven miraculous signs performed by Jesus in order to demonstrate and prove His deity. Each sign has its own profound meaning.

1. At a wedding in Cana, Jesus turned the water into wine. (See John 2:1–11.) This sign marked the transition of a John the Baptist-believer into a kingdom-believer. It marked the transition from the old wine to the new wine.

2. Jesus healed the nobleman's son in Capernaum. (See John 4:46–54.) This sign showed the importance of believing in God by faith in the authority of His Word rather than relying only on His works. It marked Jesus' authority over the limits of space and distance.

3. Jesus healed the man at the pool of Bethesda. (See John 5:1–15.) This sign symbolized the need for people to leave behind the wounds of their past and to move forward. It marked the transition away from that which had paralyzed them and was preventing them from experiencing the kingdom of God.

4. Jesus fed five thousand people with five loaves and two small fish. (See John 6:1–13.) This was a metaphor for becoming a channel through which God to multiplied and spiritually fed the multitudes. It marked Jesus' authority over the limits of quantity.

5. Jesus walked on water. (See John 6:16–21.) This marked Jesus' authority over the elements of nature.

6. Jesus healed a man blind from birth by covering his eyes with mud. (See John 9:1–7.) This illustrated the limits of religious blindness and of the Pharisaic mentality. It demonstrated how the Son of God restored spiritual vision and had authority over human misfortune.

7. Jesus raised Lazarus from the dead. (See John 11:1–45.) This symbolized that Jesus is the resurrection and the life, and that He exercises dominion over death.

The purpose of these signs was to prove that Jesus was the Messiah—the Son of God—and that He was capable of giving people eternal life, along with the ability to see, hear, and experience an intimate communion with God the Father. Each sign pointed not to a man, a temple, or an organization, but only to Jesus.

What Are Wonders?

The Greek word for "wonder" is *teras*, meaning "a prodigy, portent...miracle: performed by any one." It describes something unusual that dazzles and amazes the spectator, and its origin can be described only as a sign from heaven—a divine act.

> *Then fear came upon every soul, and many wonders and signs were done through the apostles.* (Acts 2:43)

The difference between a sign and wonder is that a sign points to something or someone specific—for example, Jesus— while a wonder appeals to the imagination, the intellect, and the heart of the observer, amazing him and leading him to receive the gospel.

This testimony illustrates an amazing wonder:

While we were worshipping and ministering at a service for ten thousand people in the Los Angeles Sports Arena, God's glory and power descended until the fire of His presence was manifested. It was so powerful that people felt like they were actually burning. Suddenly, from among the audience, a man began to jump and shout. When he arrived at the platform up front, he testified that he was a pastor who had spent the past eighteen years preaching against miracles because he did not believe in their veracity and thought they were inventions of preachers. He had not informed his congregation that he was attending this conference. I noticed that he carried a cane in his hand and asked him why this was so. He said that as a child, he had suffered with polio, which had paralyzed his left leg and damaged the muscles. Indeed, his left leg had atrophied and was much thinner than the right. It looked like a thin bone covered by layer of skin. He could not raise it or move it around.

No one had laid hands on this man. While he had been in his seat, he had begun to feel his leg grow. When he touched it, he felt muscles growing from the knee down, but it was still thin and weak from the knee up. It was then that he cried out, "Lord, finish Your work in me, please!" Instantly, he felt his leg fill in with muscle from the knee up. He began to move the leg, showing everyone his healing. This testimony was wonderful. It amazed all who were present, led hundreds to salvation, and exalted the name of Jesus. This miracle received so much attention that some in the secular news media in Los Angeles covered the event for several days afterward.

What Is the Casting Out of Demons?

The war between the kingdom of God and the kingdom of darkness is fought over the dominion of the human soul. God created us, but Satan has worked hard to destroy us because he hates God and anything that resembles Him. Satan pretends to govern the earth in order to gain lordship over the Father's most valuable possession: His children—us! When an individual refuses to welcome Jesus into his heart, the enemy takes over that place and colonizes the territory, blinding that individual and preventing him from seeing and knowing the Son of God. Satan's ultimate goal is to contaminate mankind with sin, sickness, and death, and to eternally separate us from the Father. But Jesus came to stop him and his evil works.

Two kingdoms cannot govern an individual. The casting out of demons implies the establishment of the kingdom of light, with the subsequent displacement of the kingdom of darkness. Jesus came to establish the kingdom of heaven on earth. He has the power to cast Satan out. Jesus went to hell and took the keys of death and Hades away from the devil. (See Revelation 1:18.) Then, He gave us the authority, in His name, to do the same. (See Luke 10:19.)

Thus, the casting out of demons is the act of uprooting them from a body they control on the basis of Jesus' delegated authority and the power of the Holy Spirit. In other words, to cast out a demon is to dethrone Satan and stop his control of an individual, thereby allowing the light of Jesus to shine on that person and lead him to reconciliation with the Father. This process makes the person an active member of the kingdom of heaven, taking him from death to life.

> Now John answered Him, saying, "Teacher, we saw someone who does not follow us **casting out demons** in Your name, and we forbade him because he does not follow us." But Jesus said, "Do not forbid him, for no one who works **a miracle** in My name can soon afterward speak evil of Me." (Mark 9:38–39, emphasis added)

In the verse above, we see a direct relationship between miracles and the casting out of demons. The casting out of demons is a miracle because it is a supernatural occurrence.

> And the multitudes with one accord heeded the things spoken by Philip, hearing and seeing the miracles which he did. For unclean spirits, crying with a loud voice, came out of many who were possessed; and many who were paralyzed and lame were healed. (Acts 8:6–7)

The signs mentioned in these verses were visible miracles that happened instantaneously, before the eyes of witnesses. In my years of ministry, as I have ministered the supernatural power of God, I have discovered that many illnesses are related to demonic activity in the body, emotions, and/or bloodline. Satan's plan is to kill and destroy God's creation—mankind—and this is his purpose for causing sicknesses and plagues. When we cast out demons from people, frequently, they are healed instantly. I have even witnessed this take place in those who suffer from cancer. Therefore, if we continue to cast out demons, the lame will walk and the blind will see by the signs performed.

Here is a testimony that illustrates this point:

A young lady came to the church after seeing a video on the Internet. She had spent almost all her life dealing with depression. At the age of eleven, she started to use drugs and alcohol. She often ran away from home and even tried to commit suicide seven times by cutting her wrists. Then, one day, she saw a video of our youth pastor and wrote to her. In time, this woman received deliverance from the demons that controlled her, she prayed the Sinner's Prayer, and God transformed her life. Satan was controlling her through depression, drugs, alcohol, and even the spirit of suicide, but God rescued her, and, today, she is free and loving life.

The casting out of demons is a visible manifestation of the presence of the kingdom of God.

God's supernatural power was evident in the life of the apostle Paul.

Now God worked unusual miracles by the hands of Paul.
(Acts 19:11)

For the members of the early church, miracles were an everyday, normal occurrence. During the first years of Christianity, people experienced miracles and supernatural dimensions rarely seen today. Every miracle performed by God is amazing and wonderful, but some seem to have a more dramatic effect than others.

I remember a lady who had spent eighteen years suffering from chronic hepatitis C, the most devastating type of hepatitis. She had been infected through a blood transfusion and had been treated with chemotherapy that had caused hair loss, depigmentation, weakness, depression, damaged internal organs, and a loss of memory.

The day I preached at her church, God spoke directly to her, saying that everything the devil had stolen from her would be returned. She felt a strong pressure and internal heat that seemed to enter through her head and travel down to her feet. As I prayed for her and said, "I declare life to your body!" she wasted no time and appropriated her blessing. Afterward, she went to her doctor, who confirmed that the virus was gone. The medical professionals had to acknowledge that her healing had been a miracle because they knew that there was no human cure for this disease. This was one of several miracles that took place after I spoke the word that God gave me. That day, in addition to this miracle, God also recreated a spleen that this woman had lost in a previous accident. Plus, she found that she was no longer barren, a fact that was proven when she soon became pregnant. Praise God!

Our responsibility is to present this generation with a powerful message with demonstrations of *iasis* healing, *therapeia* cures, and *iama* salvations. They need to experience *dynamis* (miracles), *semeion* (signs), and *teras* (wonders) that include the casting out of demons. These supernatural acts make up the gospel of the kingdom because they testify that Jesus lives and is available to all those who believe and desire to manifest His power as a blessing in the lives of other people. Presenting this generation with anything less is not the gospel of the kingdom.

> *Healing, miracles, signs, wonders, and the casting out of demons are keys to expanding God's kingdom on earth.*

People who personally experience a miracle exercise their faith. They do not idly stand by, waiting for something to happen. It is important to clarify that Jesus performed miracles through many different means. The Holy Spirit does not always do things the same way. Sometimes, Jesus barely touched the person. Other times, He laid hands on him or her. In other cases, He declared the Word, touched the person's ear, or made mud with His saliva. If we desire the supernatural, we must be flexible and ready to obey the Holy Spirit at a moment's notice.

Ways God Confirmed and Validated the Ministry of Jesus

- **With miracles, signs, wonders, and the gifts of the Holy Spirit**

God also bearing witness both with signs and wonders, with various miracles, and gifts of the Holy Spirit, according to His own will.... (Hebrews 2:4)

God testified concerning Jesus through four methods: miracles, signs, wonders, and the gifts of the Holy Spirit. It is important to keep in mind that, because of their culture, the Jews required signs from men who claimed to be of God. They did not acknowledge anyone as a prophet until they saw some demonstration of supernatural signs. Thus, every prophet in the Old Testament distinguished his ministry with signs and miracles. We will never reach the Jews—much less the Muslim nations—with a gospel that lacks supernatural signs and wonders. As a matter of fact, I would not go to any other country if I were not convinced that God would support my message with miracles, signs, and wonders.

This man came to Jesus by night and said to Him, "Rabbi, we know that You are a teacher come from God; for no one can do these signs that You do unless God is with him." (John 3:2)

As I've stated, everyone who operates in miracles does so by revelation, or revealed knowledge. In the presence of genuine revelation, there is no way to avoid the manifestation of miracles, which serve to confirm that the revelation came from God.

No man moves in the supernatural with a truth that does not exceed the common.

In the history of the church, everyone who has ever moved in miracles, signs, and wonders was obeying a revelation of God, which was confirmed by His Word. These men and women left their legacies on earth. They were pioneers who went ahead of their generations in order to teach its members to do the same, and to transfer their legacies to the future generations.

In the twentieth century, God raised, and continues to raise in this century, men and women with revelation. Their names are immediately associated with the power in which they operate. For instance, when I mention Pastor William Seymour, I think of revival and miracles. When I bring up A. A. Allen, I see miracles and saved souls. The same goes for Yiye Ávila. When I think of Carlos Annacondia, I think of salvation and deliverance. Omar Cabrera personifies salvation and the destruction of strongholds. Bill Hamon deals with the prophetic word, Alan Vincent with the revelation of the kingdom and spiritual warfare, Dr. T. L. Osborn with miracles, healings, prodigies, and salvation, and Morris Cerullo with miracles, salvation, and the prophetic move of the Spirit. Likewise, when I think of Apostle Cash Luna, I associate him with healing, miracles, and finances.

What if I mention other preachers? Would you be able to identify any of them? If you immediately associate them with the supernatural, it means that is their "apostolic seal"—the revelation in which they operate. Today, many people in ministry lack revelation. If all they do is manifest miracles, it is because they are using the principles they learned from others who do have revelation.

- **By approving the ministry of His Son**

   Men of Israel, hear these words: Jesus of Nazareth, a Man attested by God to you by miracles, wonders, and signs which God did through Him in your midst, as you yourselves also know. (Acts 2:22)

God approves and validates our ministries the same way He approved the ministry of His Son—with miracles, signs, and wonders.

- ## By confirming His identity as the Messiah

Jesus answered and said to them, "Go and tell John the things which you hear and see: the blind see and the lame walk; the lepers are cleansed and the deaf hear; the dead are raised up and the poor have the gospel preached to them." (Matthew 11:4–5)

These verses constitute the reply of Jesus to John the Baptist, who, after declaring Jesus to be the Messiah and the Lamb of God who takes away the sin of the world (see John 1:29), doubted the truth after he was imprisoned. The thing to admire here is that Jesus did not answer by recounting His many personal achievements or by telling John how good or holy He was. Rather, He reminded John's messenger of all the supernatural works God was doing through Him, and how this confirmed His identity as the true Messiah. These should be our credentials, as well. When people criticize, persecute, judge, or doubt our ministries and callings, we should respond with evidence—signs that prove that our ministries come from God and that we belong to Him.

What Purpose Is There in Miracles, Signs, and Wonders?

Certainly, there have been excesses and abuse in the area of miracles. This, however, should not be an obstacle to manifesting them, because those who have feared the excesses have ended up on the other extreme: living without God's power or miracles. To shed light on this matter, let us examine the biblical purpose for miracles.

- ## Miracles testify that Jesus is the Son of God.

If I do not do the works of My Father, do not believe Me; but if I do, though you do not believe Me, believe the works, that you may know and believe that the Father is in Me, and I in Him. (John 10:37–38)

God testifies the instant His Word is preached. If people fail to believe by the Word, they will believe by signs and miracles. If a miracle does not point to Jesus, I doubt that it comes from God.

We live in a generation that yearns to see the power of Jesus. Many motivational preachers deliver inspirational messages that simply meet the temporal needs of the people, but they are unable to prove with supernatural evidence that Jesus is the Son of God. When Moses spoke with Pharaoh, God supported him with powerful miracles that forced the pharaoh's hand and gave the people of Israel faith to believe that they would escape from slavery and reach the Promised Land.

It is an insult to the cross to preach a message that does not deliver. Many self-appointed leaders give themselves titles, calling themselves apostles, doctors, evangelists, and so forth. But, regardless of what titles they choose or which offices they claim to hold, they will be deemed credible only when the blind can see them and the deaf can hear them praise and worship the name of Jesus. Only this will guarantee their veracity.

- **Miracles speak an allegoric truth concerning the kingdom of God.**

  So He took the blind man by the hand and led him out of the town. And when He had spit on his eyes and put His hands on him, He asked him if he saw anything.
  (Mark 8:23)

Every time Jesus performed a miracle, it was to illustrate the spiritual condition of the people and to confirm His identity as the Son of God. For instance, when He healed the blind, He illustrated spiritual blindness. I often see this in my own ministry. I may be teaching on the kingdom, and God will heal the blind as a sign that He is giving spiritual sight to His people and enabling them to see the kingdom.

During a healing service at our church, God revealed to me that He wanted to heal the blind. When I made the call, a woman who had been blind in her right eye for thirteen years came forward. The retina in her eye had been destroyed, making it impossible for her to see. I prayed for her, and Jesus instantly healed her. I cannot express the joy and surprise that this woman experienced when she began to see people's faces with an eye that only minutes before had been totally blind. As He was doing it in the physical world, God was also restoring sight to the spiritually blind, allowing them to see what He was doing in their presence.

- **Miracles persuade people who thirst for God to seek Him.**

Some people want to perform miracles but feel they will not be able to until they develop better character. This is a traditional religious mentality because the Bible does not mention the need to have a developed character before moving in miracles. Although I consider character to be essential for living a holy life, it is not essential to perform miracles. All that is needed for miracles to happen is to do them in the name of Jesus. Signs and miracles will persuade unbelievers to run to God because they will realize that He lives, that He is real, and that He did, indeed, resurrect from the dead. Sadly, some people are desperately seeking God without success. For them, a miracle is the sign that can show them where to find the God they desperately yearn for.

- **Miracles, signs, and wonders expand and establish the kingdom in hostile territories.**

For our gospel did not come to you in word only, but also in power, and in the Holy Spirit and in much assurance.
(1 Thessalonians 1:5)

A few years ago, Miami was referred to as a "cemetery" for pastors because it was a difficult place for churches to grow and develop. For almost a generation—over forty years—churches were unable to grow beyond twenty-five hundred members. However, when we started to preach the gospel of the kingdom with demonstrations of God's power, including miracles, signs, and wonders, the city opened up. We became the fastest-growing Hispanic church in the United States, and, today, we continue to grow. We are one of the pioneering churches of Miami, and God has raised other anointed men to serve Him in other sectors of the city. At first, there was great opposition from several pastors who were not in agreement with the subject of deliverance and miracles, but God quickly testified of our veracity and confirmed that He had sent us. Many of those pastors today send men and women to our Leadership Institute to be trained and equipped to serve as leaders in their churches.

Today, our mission continues to grow and expand the kingdom of God. I believe that God has asked us to reach 12 percent of the population of Miami—He promised it. Within the infrastructure required to welcome such a great harvest, God ordained that I should build an arena for twenty thousand people, as well as an accredited Christian university that is able to serve the secular sector. The purpose of doing this is to impact the professional and Christian realms and give the leaders of our society the ability to handle the laws of both the spiritual and natural world. This has brought about growth at levels that are difficult to describe, but this growth has been a result of the miracles, signs, wonders, gifts of the Holy Spirit, and casting out of demons, all of which God has performed through His trained leadership.

- **Miracles, signs, and wonders help plant churches that grow and stand firm.**

We find this pattern in Scripture: wherever a church or ministry was planted on the foundation of the supernatural—miracles, signs, and wonders—there was rapid growth that naturally affected the entire region. In my experience with planting churches and helping others to do the same, I have observed that the keys to acceleration are evangelism, prayer, deliverance, the restoration of the family, miracles, signs, and wonders. I can testify that all the churches and ministries under my spiritual covering, in twenty-five countries around the world, have expanded their membership numbers from hundreds to thousands in a short period of time.

- **Miracles, signs, and wonders help evangelize throughout the world.**

  And this gospel of the kingdom will be preached in all the world as a witness to all the nations, and then the end will come. (Matthew 24:14)

To testify is to make something evident. This verse says, in other words, "This gospel will be proclaimed to make evident and manifest God's supernatural power to all the nations of the world." It will be a replica of the ministry of Jesus. Otherwise, it is not the gospel of the kingdom. Preaching the gospel without the evidence of miracles will not do. The world is waiting for miraculous evidence that can be seen only when the gospel of the kingdom is preached. More people can be saved in less time with supernatural evidence than without it. The gospel of the kingdom will be preached with the testimony that is supported by miracles, signs, and wonders.

Our testimony is our message. How do we know people can be delivered? Because we were made free! How do we know people can be healed? Because we were healed! We will never be credible witnesses if God does not give us personal testimonies. When we can say, "I was blind but now I see," we become a witness of Jesus—one who has seen, heard, and personally experienced God's power.

- **Miracles, signs, and wonders challenge the minds of skeptics and others who are hostile toward the gospel.**

When God manifests miracles, signs, and wonders, people are amazed and convicted. This is one way people are encouraged to change their ways and respond to the gospel. There are countries in the world where it is difficult to evangelize without the clear demonstration of miracles, which remove the veil of unbelief and sensitize the hearts of the people toward God.

- **Miracles, signs, and wonders confirm with signs the preaching of God's Word.**

And they went out and preached everywhere, the Lord working with them and confirming the word through the accompanying signs. (Mark 16:20)

In the days of Jesus, miracles, signs, and wonders always confirmed the message of the gospel of the kingdom. They were never performed out of context with the Word or to exalt a particular individual. If we have a good product, we don't have to lie to sell it because the product will speak for itself. It will become our best testimony. In this case, miracles, signs, and wonders give credibility. They penetrate the intellectual and humanistic minds that are opposed to the gospel.

- **Miracles, signs, and wonders are proof that Jesus was raised from the dead and lives forever.**

And with great power the apostles gave witness to the resurrection of the Lord Jesus. And great grace was upon them all. (Acts 4:33)

Miracles done in the name of Jesus are the supernatural evidences of His resurrection. And, if Jesus was resurrected, He will do greater things than He did while He walked the earth.

The following is a powerful testimony pointing to the fact that Jesus still lives:

On a Sunday, during a visit at one of our daughter churches in Cape Coral, Florida, the building was overflowing with people. As I ministered, God's glory descended. His presence was so powerful that it caused a beautiful new song in the Spirit to come forth, a song that silenced the atmosphere in the place. In the midst of a powerful fire of the Spirit, a woman came forth to testify, saying that she had been missing seven teeth, but that, when the glory of God had descended, she had felt heat in her mouth. When her dentist examined her later, he found that God had created seven new teeth. This was a glorious miracle!

Many miracles took place that weekend. In another case, a man who had been in an accident that had required him to get screws and metal plates in his knees began to jump up and down. When he came to the altar, he held the screws in his hands. They had fallen off, and he was totally healed!

Principles of Operating in Miracles

As you know, miracles originate in the spirit realm and manifest in the natural realm. However, you can enter the spirit realm only by faith, not through the human intellect. This fact yields the following principles:

- **To move in the supernatural, we must disconnect ourselves from reason.**

When we speak about miracles, we must keep in mind that they do not exist in the human intellect or imagination, but only in the supernatural dimension, where reason has no access. To perform miracles, we must remove all reason, because very little of what God does makes sense in the natural. If it does make sense, it probably doesn't come from God. The world's Western cultures tend to operate almost exclusively on the basis of reason. For anyone to believe, it must make sense; otherwise, they reject it. Nevertheless, God can do much more than what our human intellect is able to understand, assimilate, or reason.

The majority of what Jesus said to His disciples made little sense to them when He said it.

When we do things that make no sense, people are quick to label us as crazy. The following is a testimony that goes beyond reason:

Some time ago, God began to do the type of miracle that took me a while to obey: weight loss. During a crusade, as the Holy Spirit led me to pray for obese people, a highly emotional woman came forward to testify. She was crying and laughing at the same time. She said that she had arrived obese but was prepared with a safety pin to hold up her skirt in case she needed it—she had believed that I would be praying for obese people. Immediately after I loosened the word, she made it hers. Almost immediately, she had to hold up her skirt to keep it from falling off. In seconds, her body was reduced by approximately four dress sizes. If I had not obeyed, her miracle would not have manifested. Sometimes, what God asks us to do does not make sense, but, for the one who needs the miracle, it makes a lot of sense!

- **Under the anointing, the miracles go hand in hand with faith.**

Miracles don't happen just like that. We have to operate by the principle of faith and the anointing. God always moves in His glory by His sovereignty and His initiative. Likewise, we often have to operate by our own initiative in the anointing, the gifts, or by faith. This usually happens in places where the revelation of glory is nonexistent. We operate in miracles under the anointing, but, in the realm of glory, the miracles already exist.

- **Miracles should be everyday happenings, not isolated events.**

And through the hands of the apostles many signs and wonders were done among the people. (Acts 5:12)

In some churches, miracles take place only when a famous evangelist visits the city. This is not how it should be! Every believer has received a mandate from God, along with His *dynamis* power and *exusia* authority, to heal the sick, perform miracles, and cast out demons. This is Jesus manifesting His life through us!

- **Miracles should be declared the instant they manifest.**

By faith we understand that the worlds were framed by the word of God. (Hebrews 11:3)

In Greek, the verb *frame* means "to render...to fit, sound, complete...to mend (what has been broken or rent), to repair... equip, put in order, arrange, adjust." Therefore, according to this verse, our faith tells us that the universe was rendered, fit, completed, mended, repaired, equipped, ordered, arranged, and adjusted by the Word of God. Major manifestations of God's supernatural power are evident today, but the only ones that remain are those that are declared and confirmed. Some people receive miracles but never testify of them. This causes them to lose their miracles a short time later. When a miracle is not declared, its presence in the natural realm becomes illegal. Healing and the miracle of deliverance will not remain unless we testify to them.

Miracles must be received and declared; otherwise, they will not stay.

One Sunday, I was ministering in our church during one of our special services that we call "Nights of Supernatural Power." During the service, there was a man who had very little hair on his head. While we worshipped, God's glory descended, flooding the temple with His presence. Suddenly, the gentleman sitting behind this bald man began to see hair grow on his head at an incredible speed. As soon as the "bald" man realized this, he stood up and ran to the front to testify. God, in His sovereignty and glory, had performed an instant miracle in this man. But it did not end there, because God continues to perform this healing in other men and women in our congregation. To prove the veracity of their testimony, they often show me their driver's license photos, in which they appear bald.

These are creative miracles that remain, thanks to the power of testimony. The condition for a miracle to remain is to verbally declare it. I once asked God why so few miracles take place among His people if His presence is so strong and belongs to everyone. God's answer was that miracles are always taking place, but people fail to declare and testify to them. Therefore, we must testify and declare our miracles!

- **We were educated to adapt to the natural reality and not to miracles.**

Our reality is determined by the natural dimension. If something miraculous happens, it is hard to understand because it is seen as an isolated event. This has to change. We must reach the point of total persuasion and conviction that God is supernatural and that He continues to perform miracles. This has nothing to do with "talking up" God but rather seeing and acknowledging His manifested presence. If God cannot heal the sick or perform miracles, then we must stop calling Him God. If the supernatural offends people, it is because they don't know Him. God cannot be defined without acknowledging the supernatural within Him. If something out of the ordinary takes place, why does the church feel the need to have meetings and debates in order to explain it away? Why do people always need to decide for themselves whether or not something is from God? We must be fully convicted that He is a supernatural God who continues to perform miracles according to His will.

Men criticize everything they cannot produce.

God always manifests His will by doing extraordinary things. The following account will testify to this:

During a service at our daughter church in Orlando, Florida, a lady came forward who had had a hysterectomy because of a four-centimeter cyst that the doctors had found in her uterus. Her menstrual cycle had not been active in the three years since the operation. But the moment the glory of God descended upon her body, she accepted her healing. The next day, her menstrual cycle restarted. When she returned to the doctor, they performed an ultrasound. To their surprise, she had a new uterus! This miracle left the doctors amazed and perplexed, unable to explain what had happened. They had the medical evidence that proved this lady had no uterus, but now, they had evidence to the contrary. The Lord had created a new organ within her in the midst of His presence.

- **Miracles exist in the *now,* not in time.**

Jesus never prayed for a sick person, but He did declare the Word in the present, with power and authority. He would say, "Be healed," or "Be free," because He realized that the kingdom of God had already come. Jesus essentially said, "Your miracle is now!" He continually broke the laws of time, space, and matter.

Some preachers prophesy miracles for the future. As a result, their people seek healing only and not miracles. Other pastors have caused miracles to be delayed because they speak of them only in the future tense, saying, "God *will* create a miracle," or "God *will* bring a revival," or "God *will* visit us with His glory." Rarely do they declare what God is doing and saying *now.* Perhaps some people would not have died had someone proclaimed the miracles that are available today! It is good to clarify that even if a miracle does not manifest immediately in the physical, it can still be received in the spirit in that particular moment!

Faith is for now! This is the principle required to receive your miracle.

Most of the men and women who received or performed a miracle in the Bible broke the laws of time. For instance:

- **The Syro-Phoenician woman**

Then Jesus answered and said to her, "O woman, great is your faith! Let it be to you as you desire." And her daughter was healed from that very hour.　　(Matthew 15:28)

Jesus had told this woman that it was not her time because He had not yet died or been resurrected. So, how did she receive her healing? I believe it was because Jesus entered the spirit realm by faith, went to the foundation of the world, and brought her daughter's healing into the now.

- **Lazarus**

[Martha] *said to* [Jesus], *"Yes, Lord, I believe that You are the Christ, the Son of God, who is to come into the world."....Jesus said to her, "Did I not say to you that if you would believe you would see the glory of God?"*
(John 11:27, 40)

Jesus lived in the power of God in *the now*; Martha spoke only of His future resurrection. Jesus had to surpass her intellect and reason in order to lead her into eternity, where everything is in the *now*, the eternal present. That is where Jesus went to get Lazarus and bring him into a new life.

Most believers have a future mentality, not a now mentality.

The following testimony demonstrates that miracles exist in the now rather than the future:

During a healing service in Maracaibo, Venezuela, one of the pastors from our church prayed for a woman who had lost the use of her right ankle due to an automobile accident six months prior. Her foot looked as though it was hanging from her lower leg, and she suffered from intense pain that kept her from walking, even with the help of a crutch. As soon as the pastor prayed for her, the Lord did a creative miracle and gave her a new ankle in front of the multitudes. The woman shouted with joy and began to run and jump all over the church. She affirmed that while they were praying for her, she had felt a strong pull in the bone of her leg and an intense heat throughout her body. It was then that she had realized that she could put weight on her foot. She had received her creative miracle! She no longer needed an ankle transplant. God had given her a new one! The woman was completely healed. Today, she walks normally and is happy and grateful to God for her miracle.

Who Can Operate in the Flow of Miracles?

- **Believers who change their mentality by revelation and the wisdom of the Holy Spirit**

That the God of our Lord Jesus Christ, the Father of glory, may give to you the spirit of wisdom and revelation in the knowledge of Him. (Ephesians 1:17)

God gives us revelation when we have renewed our minds according to His thoughts. Then, He gives us the concepts, such as "how." When the Spirit of wisdom and revelation is absent, it is replaced by "common information." Many Christians believe in miracles but have no idea how to operate in them because they lack revelation. Each revelation given by God includes the way or method to carry it out because the Spirit of wisdom is in it. Some people base their works on information rather than revelation. As a result, they have an absence of manifestations of God. When miracles are in place, it is rare for God to do anything without the cooperation of a believer. Remember, He operates through you and me. We cannot do anything if God does not tell us how to do it. If we don't know the "how," how will we do it?

- **Believers who believe**

And these signs will follow those who believe: in My name they will cast out demons; they will speak with new tongues; they will take up serpents; and if they drink anything deadly, it will by no means hurt them; they will lay hands on the sick, and they will recover. (Mark 16:17–18)

Note that this passage says that the signs *"will follow those who believe."* It does not say that they "will follow only the preacher or pastor." It seems that very few of the signs noted in Mark 16 follow today's believers, mostly due to unbelief.

"Go into all the world and preach the gospel to every crea-ture" (verse 15). The Greek word for *"go"* is *poreu,* meaning "to lead over, carry over, transfer...to pursue the journey on which one has entered, to continue on one's journey." We will never be used to perform miracles with God's supernatural power if we don't dare to go, or journey, and gather the harvest.

To *"go"* implies continuous action. In other words, every-where we go, whether on an airplane or a bus, we should be about our mission of healing the sick. The Greek word derives from another word that means "beyond, on the other side." This implies a penetration or piercing. It requires a voluntary action, but God also does His part as we go. What I want us to under-stand is that as we go, we become channels of God's power. I have great passion to see my city, as well as all the nations of the world, transformed through signs, wonders, and miracles produced by His power.

- **Believers who become a sign**

Here am I and the children whom the LORD has given me! We are for signs and wonders in Israel from the LORD of hosts. (Isaiah 8:18)

When we seek Jesus, not only will signs follow us, but we will also *become* a sign. This is conditional, however, because signs will follow us only if we go. If we remain rooted, noth-ing will follow us. We are the living, genuine testimony of the wonderful work of Jesus Christ in our lives, through which He saved us, transformed us, forgave us, and made us to become a sign for the whole world to see that He lives and can save and change anyone who humbly and wholeheartedly seeks Him.

- **Believers who move in supernatural boldness**

Grant to Your servants that with all boldness they may speak Your word. (Acts 4:29)

Jesus is as much the miracle-maker today as He was when He walked the earth. Humanity needs a touch of His miraculous power as never before. Wherever a man of God demonstrates his supernatural boldness and faith in God's Word, healing, miracles, signs, and wonders will take place, and people will be drawn to Christ.

Personally, I refuse to preach a gospel without miracles. What type of Bible would we have if it were not full of miracles? What type of message would we preach if it never manifested miracles as evidence of its veracity? What types of preachers speak against miracles?

The message of the gospel of the kingdom, accompanied by supernatural evidence of its veracity, must be taken and preached to all the nations of the world in order to gather the harvest. Our testimony, accompanied by supernatural evidence, convicts people and is more effective than any philosophical lecture. A miracle is better than a thousand empty sermons. People are desperate to know and serve the God of miracles. Every social stratum, race, profession, and office has the same desire to know the truth and is ready to accept Jesus when miracles appear. You and I—believers—are God's agents, His representatives on earth, anointed by Jesus to do the same miracles and signs He performed.

Every believer can move in miracles, signs, and wonders, because they are available to everyone who preaches the gospel—the revelation that Jesus lives and will manifest Himself through us when we surrender our pride and humble ourselves. He lives and is ready to continue performing miracles. He wants to use our humanity so that we can become channels of blessings through signs and wonders.

If you need a miracle of healing, I want to pray for you now, declaring that while you read this book, you will be healed:

Father, in the name of Jesus, I order every person who is sick or needs a creative miracle in his or her body—a new organ or physical healing—to be healed at this moment. I order every person to be healed, delivered, and transformed right now! Furthermore, I ask for those who are skeptics and need a visible sign of Your supernatural power to receive a miracle. I further declare that everything covered in this book will manifest in visible and tangible ways in their lives. Perform a miracle, manifest Your signs, and show them a wonder as they read, so they will believe that Jesus is the Son of God, that He lives, and that He loves them. Amen.

Summary

- I have seen Jesus perform miracles through me and other people.

- A healing is a progressive work of God's supernatural power.

- A miracle is the instant work of God's supernatural power, the divine interruption of the natural laws of time, space, and matter.

- A sign is something that points to something or someone for the purpose of giving direction or destiny.

- Jesus performed seven signs that affirmed His identity as the Son of God: He turned the water into wine, healed the nobleman's son in Capernaum, healed the lame man in Bethesda, fed five thousand, walked on water, healed the man blind from birth, and raised Lazarus from the dead.

- A marvel is something that amazes the spectator and testifies of Jesus while appealing to the imagination, intellect, and heart.

- The casting out of demons is the uprooting of the enemy from the souls or spirits of people in the name of Jesus and by the power of His Spirit in order to establish the kingdom of God in them and to give them eternal life.

- God confirmed and validated the ministry of Jesus with four things: miracles, signs, wonders, and the gifts of the

Holy Spirit. By them, God publicly approved Jesus and His ministry and confirmed His identity as the Messiah.

- The purposes of miracles, signs, and wonders are to testify of Jesus as the Son of God, to speak an allegorical truth concerning the kingdom, to persuade people to seek God, to expand and establish the kingdom, to plant churches, to spread the gospel worldwide, to challenge the intellect of skeptics, to confirm the preaching of the Word, and to prove that Jesus lives.

- The following are needed to operate in miracles: a disconnection from reason; an alignment of miracles with our level of faith; a belief that miracles are the norm, not the exception; the will to declare miracles as soon as they manifest; an adaptation to the supernatural realm; and an acknowledgment that miracles exist in the *now*, not in time.

- A mind renewed by revelation and the wisdom of the Spirit are the only things needed to perform miracles. We must be full of the Spirit of wisdom, we must believe, we must become a sign, and we must have supernatural boldness.

9

Principles, Concepts, and Revelations for Operating in the Supernatural

This is one of the most useful chapters of this book. Here, I will share the principles, concepts, and revelations I have learned over my twenty years of experience in ministering the supernatural power of God to thousands of people. This chapter is the result of my having seen God perform all kinds of healings, deliverances, transformations, salvations, miracles, signs, and wonders. In addition, I want to share what I have learned over the years from other men and women of God who also exercise this power. I want you to know the concepts, principles, and fundamentals that will make you desire more of His power until your passion leads you to experience the supernatural power of God in your life.

1. It is crucial to maintain a personal prayer life that perseveres continually.

Now it came to pass, as He was praying in a certain place, when He ceased, that one of His disciples said to Him, "Lord, teach us to pray." (Luke 11:1)

Jesus was praying with His disciples, but only one asked Him to teach them to pray. It seems that in those days, as well as today, believers had a difficult time understanding the importance of personal and corporate prayer. Perhaps Peter asked this because he understood that all of the healings and other miraculous works of Jesus were made possible by His prayer life. Indeed, Jesus' continuous and persistent prayer life was the main force behind all the miracles, signs, and wonders He performed. Furthermore, prayer directly connected Jesus to the power and authority to deliver the oppressed by casting out their demons. Jesus spent hours in close intimacy with the Father, which empowered the seconds He spent healing the sick and afflicted and raising the dead.

Hours spent with God turn into
minutes spent with men.

Jesus' Prayer Life...

- opened the heavens.

- caused God's power to be manifested everywhere He went.

- helped Him to choose His disciples.

- filled Him with the power to heal the masses and deliver them from demons. Jesus did not pray in front of people for a healing—He simply declared the word. Because of His intimacy with the Father, He had already won the battle and held their healing in His hands.

- caused God's power to permeate His body and clothing, with the result being that people were healed by His mere touch.

- produced authority and the anointing for the disciples to heal the sick. They did not carry the message of the kingdom under their own anointing but under the anointing produced by the prayer life of Jesus. Likewise, today, many move under the anointing generated by another person's life of prayer, someone who may be in authority over them. Because of this, even a new believer can perform miracles.

- revealed Jesus' true identity to the disciples.

- awakened within His disciples a deep desire to pray. This is reported in the book of Acts, which illustrates that they never made a decision without seeking the counsel of the Holy Spirit in prayer.

- taught the disciples the need and the power of persisting in prayer.

- produced zeal for God's house.

- kept Peter's faith from failing in the midst of a trial.

- led Jesus to fight and win the war against death. Thanks to His life of prayer, He obtained the resurrection even before going to the cross.

Jesus' prayer life, and His intimate relationship with the Father, produced a supernatural atmosphere to loosen miracles and cast out demons everywhere He went. I can testify that all men of God who walk in the supernatural "walk on their knees." This is the key to the success of Jesus' ministry on earth, a success I apply to my life every day. I know what it is to be in the presence of God for hours before a service, studying His Word, praising and worshipping, and waiting on Him. During this time spent in His presence, the Holy Spirit gives me instruction on what He wants to do with His people and how He wants to do it during each service. He also shows me the direction in which He wants to take the church. I always write down His instructions—when He wants to heal certain types of sicknesses, when He wants to baptize in the Holy Spirit, or when He gives me specific prophetic words.

A clear example of this is found in the following testimony:

One day, I preached at one of our daughter churches, Little Havana, in downtown Miami, Florida. For many years, the pastors of the church had been searching for a new building in an area where it was difficult to find one that was satisfactory. However, God gave me a prophetic word that said and within six months, they would own their building. A few months later, that word was confirmed. What had taken years, God provided in months. What made this happen? I believe it was the time I spent in God's presence, studying His Word. Time spent with God produces prophecy, healing, miracles, and all the fruits you see through this ministry.

2. Corporate prayer and intercession are just as important as personal prayer.

Another necessity of operating in the supernatural is the atmosphere produced by corporate prayer and worship, as well as the intercession of a church or community that loosens God's presence to perform miracles and healing.

God has blessed me with a wife who has a strong calling for prayer and intercession. Over a period of about fourteen years, she fully developed a ministry of intercession in our church. She begins each day at three in the morning and prays until seven alongside an army of intercessors who accompany her without apprehension. Personal and corporate prayer are the keys that have created the supernatural atmosphere that rests upon our ministry. Apostles and prophets who visit always comment on the atmosphere, saying that it seems saturated with God's presence, and that anything could happen at any time. If we are visited by a prophet, prayer makes it easier for him or her to enter into God's presence and loosen the prophetic message for me, our church, or our leadership. If we are visited by an apostle, when he brings forth a revelation, miracles and healings occur.

I believe these things occur because the atmosphere of our church is built on the continuous prayer and intercession of my wife, Ana, and her God-given team of intercessors. I can testify to this because it is common for me to preach and experience God's presence—for the blind to see, the deaf-mute to hear and speak, the lame to walk; for cancer to disappear; and for all types of miracles to take place. When I travel to other countries, I can feel the support of their prayers and intercession over my life and the lives of the team members who accompany me. Wherever we go, we carry the atmosphere of our church. Thus, supernatural power is loosened in the nations.

Today, we have intercessors and musicians who pray, praise, and worship God together with the people for twenty-four hours a day. This edifies God's throne and produces supernatural manifestations that demonstrate His power and glory.

3. It is necessary to have revelation, or revealed knowledge, and God's wisdom.

That the God of our Lord Jesus Christ, the Father of glory, may give to you the spirit of wisdom and revelation in the knowledge of Him. (Ephesians 1:17)

Another necessity to operate in the supernatural is God's revealed knowledge. In the Spirit realm, we must learn to flow with the channels of spiritual access because natural channels are inoperable there. To what was Paul referring when he spoke of *"the spirit of wisdom and revelation in the knowledge of Him"*? He was referring to the fact that the spirit of wisdom and revelation teaches us how to flow in the supernatural. Many miracles remain unused in eternity because they cannot manifest until their "how" is known. Has God ever asked you to do something but you didn't know how? If we don't know the principle, it is impossible to have access to the supernatural through only logic or common sense. Remember, to gain entry into the supernatural, we need faith and revealed knowledge by the Holy Spirit. Only revelation gives us access to the spirit realm. If God does not give us a revelation, we will not have access to what the apostle Paul described as things the *"eye has not seen, nor ear heard"* (1 Corinthians 2:9). To enter into the supernatural, it takes more than confessing and declaring, more than believing or personal effort. There is no access without revelation.

Without revelation, there is no access to the supernatural. If we don't have access, it is because we don't have faith to possess it.

The supernatural does not work for those who have not received the knowledge to activate it because access is not available.

Thus, they have no right to receive it or to have it manifest. Many revivals in this country and throughout the world have died due to a lack of continuous revelation of what was to come. This lack will cause people to become stagnant. After a time, the revival turns into maintenance services where nothing new ever happens. Eventually, this happens in almost every revival because the revelation of the Holy Spirit stops.

When you receive an impartation without revelation, it cannot remain in your spirit.

How Does the Spirit of Wisdom Work?

Most Christians will say that they believe in miracles. So, why can't they flow in them? It is because they lack revelation, which, combined with the spirit of wisdom, gives access to the supernatural. Those who receive the spirit of wisdom know *how* to manifest the signs of God's power.

An example is Dr. Oral Roberts, whom I met and visited on several occasions during the sunset of his life. This man, who laid hands on more than one million people, shared with me one of his revelations. He said that whenever he was about to minister, he would lock himself in his room beforehand to pray and seek the face of God. He would not leave until he could feel God's power in his right hand. Only then did he know that he was ready for the sick to be healed. According to this principle, his hand had been anointed to heal the sick. That was the *how* God had shown him. Of course, it will not always happen the same way for everyone, but it does begin to help us to understand that there is a *how* that God's revelation will give us.

If there is an absence of revealed knowledge, or revelation, there will be no impartation or progress of faith.

For each revelation God gives, He will work something new. This is why it is so important for people to learn the *how*. There are few principles of the spirit realm operating in the church today because of a lack of revelation and an absence of the spirit of wisdom.

On the other hand, the world has its own principles, and it knows *how* to behave within the natural realm. The world collects information, performs experiments, uses trial and error, and develops concepts and practices that can be transferred to future generations through education and practical application.

No leader can take you where he has never been or beyond his knowledge.

Revelation is the prerequisite for manifestation, just as hearing is the prerequisite for faith. (See Romans 10:17.) We cannot move in the present dimension of faith without a present revelation. Therefore, if we have no revelation, we shouldn't try it.

The Son can do nothing of Himself, but what He sees the Father do; for whatever He does, the Son also does in like manner. (John 5:19)

You cannot have faith to do that which you don't know how to do.

My Experience with Revelation

In my own experience, I have noticed that God cannot manifest in a ministry beyond the revelation, or knowledge, the ministry has acquired. Some time ago, I taught in a church about knowing God as our Provider. The Lord manifested as the Provider, and many financial debts were supernaturally cancelled. God provided work, and new businesses flourished. Several transactions were successfully closed, young people received college scholarships, and court cases were resolved in favor of the faithful.

I have noticed that every time I share revealed knowledge concerning God's power, He manifests with miracles. When I teach on a specific topic, He manifests on that topic. This, of course, stresses the importance of teaching on all the areas concerning God. If we have only a minimal revelation of God, then, His manifestation will also be minimal. If we want God to manifest in any area, we must first have the revelation.

As it has now been revealed by the Spirit to His holy apostles and prophets.... (Ephesians 3:5)

Apostles and prophets bring revelation. Without them, the church is limited to basic doctrine.

In most cases, whatever a particular church knows today is due to the ministries of the pastor, evangelist, and teacher exclusively. The result is that the fundamental doctrine of Christianity is limited, because these offices often do not include such important aspects as apostolic revelation—revelation for *now*. Apostolic revelation breaks new ground by declaring what the Father is saying and doing at this moment in time. This causes the heavens to loosen what God has authorized for earth. When the Holy Spirit reveals something through the apostles and prophets, heaven can no longer contain it. It must be released!

To move in God's supernatural power, we need a continually fresh revelation. We need to hear, see, and perceive in the Spirit. Furthermore, we must know how and when to take action. Miracles do not happen by chance. We must learn to bring them forth.

For example, I have been in services in which God's presence and power were not felt. But this does not mean nothing happened. In my case, I must do what God has commanded me to do. I will pray for people, declare the work of Jesus on the cross, and watch miracles take place. This is called activating the faith, or walking in faith under the anointing. We must learn to exercise our faith.

Do you want to begin walking by faith in order to be used in miracles? Then, consider the following testimony and begin walking under its anointing.

At a healing service in Los Angeles, California, one miracle stands out among all the rest. A young man had a painful degenerative disease that compromised his bones and extremities, blocking his growth. Every time the young man tried to walk, it was a painful process because his feet were malformed. That night, while this young man was worshipping God, declaring His Word, and obeying His instructions, God's glory powerfully descended upon him and healed him. His feet were straightened, allowing him to begin to walk and even run without pain. Needless to say, I will never forget the look on this young man's face when he realized that God had healed him.

4. Thanksgiving, praise, and worship to God are vital.

But You are holy, enthroned in the praises of Israel.
(Psalm 22:3)

Another essential practice to flow in the supernatural is praise, which, in the above verse, is the translation from the Hebrew word *tehillah*, which means "a praise, song or hymn of praise...adoration, thanksgiving (paid to God)." It is a joyful hymn that praises the powerful deeds of our Lord. Another word in that verse is *"enthroned,"* which is translated from the Hebrew word *yashab*, meaning "to dwell, remain, sit, abide...to cause to sit." This makes it clear that God wants more than to just pay us a visit. He wants to stay, to get comfortable, and to govern His people who rejoice in His victories. And yet, this can occur only after thanksgiving, praise, and worship. Only when we build a throne with these three elements will God manifest among us.

Many believers think that praying means spelling out a list of petitions for God to answer, but the truth is that without thanksgiving, praise, and worship, we will never have access to God. This is the only condition by which we may enter into His presence and receive the answers to our prayers. Each of these three activities is a particular way to approach God and can help us to relate to Him on different levels. In thanksgiving, we recognize His goodness; in praise, we recognize His greatness and amazing works; and, in worship, we recognize His majesty, sovereignty, and glory.

What Is Thanksgiving?

Enter into His gates with thanksgiving, and into His courts with praise. Be thankful to Him, and bless His name.
(Psalm 100:4)

The Word of God teaches that we must always give thanks for everything, and that our petitions must always accompany thanksgiving. Some try to gain access to God by using other methods, but that won't work. Gratitude and thanksgiving are the keys to loosening God's supernatural power because they build a place—a throne—where God can dwell among us.

What Is Praise?

Praise is the proclamation and declaration of God's powerful deeds, which are articulated with jubilee, excitement, loud sounds, music, applause, shouts, and dance. To praise is to exalt God in a brilliant, extravagant celebration with powerful sounds that border on the ridiculous. It also makes us look like people who have lost their heads and their good sense. Note that this concept of praise has nothing to do with the mechanical, uniform, monotonous ways in which praise is expressed in many churches, where neither the life nor the joy of God is on display. Biblically speaking, praise is a celebration that breaks all barriers, making it able to penetrate a hostile environment.

If we want to experience deep worship, we need vibrant praise. It is the only way to see God's glory manifest.

What Is Worship?

The Hebrew word for "worship" in the Old Testament is *shachah*, which means "to bow down, prostrate oneself...before superior in homage...before God." It is an act of reverence and humiliation. In the New Testament, the Greek word for "worship" is *proskyneo*, which comes from the words *pros*, meaning "to the advantage of," and *kyon*, meaning "to kiss, like a dog licking his master's feet." With this in mind, worship, or *proskyneo*, is bowing down in respect and reverence and kissing the hands and feet of a superior. It is the ultimate expression of submission and reverence for the purpose of humbly begging someone to do something. It is comparable to a dog licking its master's hand as a demonstration of its affection.

> *Then she came and worshipped Him, saying, "Lord, help me!"* (Matthew 15:25)

Worship, then, is a humble, respectful attitude and reverence to God demonstrated by physical acts expressed through unselfish and sacrificial service. Some believe that the only difference between praise and worship is one of rhythm. They believe that one is up-tempo, while the other has a slower beat. Yet this is not the case. Praise proclaims God's powerful works, while worship offers Him humble reverence for who He is.

Praise recognizes God's powerful works while worship acknowledges the person of God.

Both the Old and New Testaments describe the posture of the body when praising and worshipping. It has nothing to do with what we say but with the attitude in which we say it. Praise and worship go beyond physical posture. They are an attitude of the spirit, body, and soul. Some physical acts used in worship are bowing the head, raising the hands, extending the arms, kneeling, and lying prostrate—facedown on the ground. These postures express that we depend totally on God, that we cannot do anything in our strength, and that, without His grace, we are lost. Once we have thanked, praised, and worshipped God, His glory will descend. His presence is the sign of His habitation, and that the throne upon which He sits has been edified.

Then Abram fell on his face, and God talked with him.
(Genesis 17:3)

The greatest act of worship is to lie facedown, prostrate before God.

How Much Time Should We Devote to Worship?

Praise until the spirit of worship descends; worship until His glory manifests.

What keeps God's presence from manifesting? It is our lack of sufficient worship. It is because we fail to build His throne with our meaningless singing and our incorrect attitudes. If worship is done in an improper or incorrect manner, God's glory will not descend. On the other hand, when we build God's throne with our worship, Satan cannot remain near us.

Let us look at a series of concepts concerning praise and worship and how to connect with the flow of the supernatural.

- **Praise and worship cause God to manifest.**

And one cried to another and said: "Holy, holy, holy is the Lord of hosts; the whole earth is full of His glory!" And the posts of the door were shaken by the voice of him who cried out, and the house was filled with smoke.

(Isaiah 6:3–4)

When we praise wholeheartedly, we incite God to reveal Himself, as He did in Scripture. In the verse above, when God was worshipped, He revealed His glory. Today, many churchgoers arrive late, missing the time of praise and worship. They attend only to hear the message, many considering themselves to be so spiritual that they don't need to worship. How will God speak to them if they don't worship first? Worship loosens the seals of revelation. When worship does not reach God's throne, revelation cannot take place. Also, when the amount of worship is lacking, the prophetic will be limited in the revelation they receive, and, as a result, creative miracles will not take place. One reason the Bible compares the Word to a hammer (see Jeremiah 23:29) is that, in some places, the atmosphere is so hard to break through that it must be hammered away. But this occurs only when there is insufficient or ineffective worship.

God reveals Himself through worship, which means that true worship is evidence that God is among us, manifesting His presence. When man fails to worship, something is wrong with him. When he can't find God, he will passionately seek to worship other created things, including idols or other human beings.

- **Worship in spirit and in truth takes place when we are no longer aware of ourselves but only of God.**

God is Spirit, and those who worship Him must worship in spirit and truth. (John 4:24)

Worship is a mandate. It has nothing to do with how we feel. Some pastors consider themselves to be too important to participate during the worship time in the service. They wait while others prepare the atmosphere. Genuine worship is complete when we forget ourselves and focus only on God. We are not worshipping God when we are thinking about ourselves and our circumstances. If we are continually worried about what other people think of us, we are not worshipping. If we continue to occupy our minds with the concerns of our day, we are not worshipping. On the contrary, we have made ourselves into a type of idol before God's presence.

- **Worship reveals where God is: a place called *there*.**

  Surely the LORD is in this place, and I did not know it.
  (Genesis 28:16)

If we want to know where God is, we must worship Him *there*—wherever we are. The Word says, *"Where two or three are gathered together in My name, I am **there**"* (Matthew 18:20, emphasis added).

Jacob also found such a place. The desert was the *there* where God met with His people. (See Genesis 28:10–16.) In Adam's case, the garden of Eden was *there*. (See Genesis 2.) The Lord makes a divine appointment with us and names the place. When we find that place—our *there*—through worship, we will see what He is doing and hear what He is saying.

There is the place where you meet with God through worship.

- **The level of praise and worship determines the type of miracles that will take place in a service.**

If the praise and worship you offer are not enough, someone with a headache may receive healing, but not someone with terminal cancer. Although there are services in which the level of praise and worship is greater than others, we must always strive to raise our level if we want to see His glory.

Also, when we praise and worship God but our lifestyle is not holy, we will not be able to ascend into His presence because we are weighted down. Anything that is not aligned with God will be a weight keeping us from rising to higher levels of worship. The Bible calls this weight *sin*.

Let us lay aside every weight, and the sin which so easily ensnares us. (Hebrews 12:1)

In the spirit realm, sin is considered spiritual gravity.

There are levels of God's presence to which some people might not be able to ascend regardless of how much they jump, crawl, shout, or prostrate themselves. If they are not ready to let go of the weight of their sin, they will never ascend. This is the reason why some people enter into God's presence faster than others. Some never enter due to the weight of their sin. No church service should regress to a previous, lower level of worship.

We cannot live on yesterday's glory. The higher we rise, the greater His glory.

While preaching in Maracaibo, Venezuela, I was surprised by a miracle that took place due to one woman's holy persistence. This woman traveled to the United States on the basis of faith, having heard from God that if I prayed for her she would be healed. Unfortunately, on the day she arrived in Miami, I was away on vacation. Not to be denied, she tried again. This time, she came to a video recording I was doing as host for TBN's *Praise the Lord*. Once again, however, she arrived just after I had left the studio. Relentless in her pursuit of God's miracle, when she heard that I would be traveling to Maracaibo, she gave it one more shot and flew to Venezuela. By the time we finally met— after her seven hours of travel—she was wheelchair-bound and unable to speak due to the cancer that had spread throughout her body, including her brain. I asked her husband to bring her to the healing crusade where God would heal her. During the worship time at the crusade, I started to preach about praise and worship. I had not yet prayed for anyone at that point when, suddenly, this woman rose to her feet and immediately began to walk and speak normally! This miracle was a direct result of God's glory descending due to His people's passionate praise and worship. In the midst of this glorious atmosphere, this woman instantly received complete healing.

Some people are more aware of their own circumstances than they are of Jesus.

- **The main reason we worship is to seek intimacy for the purpose of producing life.**

If our worship cannot produce life, it is dead. Worship is an intimate relationship, much like that between a husband and wife. My children were born as a result of the intimacy between my wife and me. It was not a chance encounter. It was planned and intentional, and two lives were created because of it. Worship, too, is planned and intentional. But if our worship is based on God's love, why do we need to be told to sing and raise our hands?

Too much of what takes place during worship in the church today has to do with the soul. It is a worship that produces emotions but too often fails to touch the spirit. Too many of the songs we sing—be they traditional, cultural, or contemporary—center on our earthly needs. When the needs of the earthly realm become our god, our worship becomes idolatry. Worship should reveal God's existence, not satisfy our own flesh. This type of impotent worship is based on our selfish human attitudes. It lacks revealed knowledge and is unable to produce miracles.

Our worship will always be linked to the revelation we have of God. We cannot praise someone we don't know. We can worship only what we know. The more intimate our knowledge of God, the more details we will have to acknowledge Him and His worth. For this reason, some believers are incapable of praising and worshipping God for long periods of time. They run out of words and stamina because they don't know whom they are worshipping. Some grow angry when the praise and worship segment of a church service lasts an hour. They consider it to be a waste of time. If they truly knew Jesus, they would be able to fix their eyes on Him during worship and forget time, circumstances, and personal needs. When we center on Jesus, He will be enthroned over our needs.

- **Praise and worship release the atmosphere of glory and God's presence.**

When we enjoy a time of intimacy with God, His plans will be birthed. If praise prepares the terrain for the type of worship in which we join Him, we will not be content to sing four dead songs and pretend to enter into His presence with bored expressions on our faces. If we are worshippers in spirit and in truth, we will edify His throne and build a dwelling place that God can inhabit among our new songs. This type of worship will heal the sick, create miracles, transform lives, and glorify God, thereby producing new life in each person at our services.

5. We must build a spiritual atmosphere.

Each time I preach or minister healing and miracles, I do so in an atmosphere produced by my life of prayer and worship and the church's corporate worship. God has always spoken from the cloud of His glory. Thus, it is important that we know how to build a spiritual atmosphere.

What Is Atmosphere?

In science, atmosphere is the layer of gases surrounding a planet. Spiritually speaking, it is the area that surrounds the believer. Spiritual atmosphere is the cloud of God's presence that surrounds us. On cold days, if you go outside, you can see your breath when you exhale. In other words, you can see the atmosphere produced by your breath. Praise and worship produce the breath of God in our midst—and His breath gives life.

We must create a celestial atmosphere for miracles, healings, and wonders to take place, an ambiance where we are able to see the words we speak. Sometimes, people will fixate on things in which faith cannot operate. If this happens, change the atmosphere or ambiance.

When Jesus left Nazareth, it was not to prove a theological point or to demonstrate that He was the Son of God. Jesus left because the atmosphere was wrong. (See Mark 6:5–6.) Many people are dying in places where the supernatural is nonexistent, where neither the life nor the presence of God can be experienced because a divine atmosphere was never generated. Prayer and intercession are not practiced, and the praise and worship are insufficient to build the tabernacle where God's glory can manifest. Because I have experienced this, I made it a point to hire full-time, professional musicians full of the Holy Spirit and taught them to manifest God's glory and to flow with me in the supernatural. Today, they know how to build an atmosphere in which God's presence can manifest so that miracles can happen. They do this in our church and everywhere else they go.

Worship establishes the divine atmosphere on earth.

From God's perspective, everything that is stuck on earth is due to the fall of man. In the beginning, heaven and earth were as one, but, when man sinned, a separation took place—a dislodging. The glory of God no longer manifested in the natural realm. The only way to bring it back is through praise and worship. Understanding this leads us to the realization that we cannot rush praise or worship during services. The duration of praise and worship depends on the place. If the atmosphere is hard to pierce, it will take longer to build the throne. Where the atmosphere already exists, one can go directly into worship.

Three Important Revelations Concerning the Spiritual Atmosphere:

- We must perceive or discern the atmosphere in any given place.
- We must loosen and declare what we perceive in the atmosphere.
- We must take and receive what is loosened in that atmosphere.

During a crusade in Mexico, I perceived that the atmosphere was not yet ready. There was a spiritual dryness that was easily perceived. This is why I always take my own musicians with me to other nations. As we began to praise and worship God, the atmosphere suddenly changed. People who had at first been detached spectators were raising their hands and allowing themselves to become broken in God's presence. It is often a matter of not only building the atmosphere but also discerning the type of atmosphere that existed there previously—whether it was one for miracles, healing, and deliverance, or for something else. As we discern this, the next step is to speak into that atmosphere in order to make what we declare come to pass.

Let us learn from this testimony how we can discern the atmosphere and how God works miracles according to His will:

During the same service in Mexico, God showed me that there were many people present who were suffering from bone problems. So, I called for them to come forward. In truth, there were people actually missing bones. Many came to the altar limping, on crutches, or in wheelchairs. Others came who had had screws surgically implanted in their bones. Because the atmosphere was ready, I declared and loosened what I knew was in that atmosphere and began to pray for those people. Specifically, I prayed for the conditions that God had shown me. I discerned the type of atmosphere we were in. In the crowd of people who came forward to declare their healings was a woman whose friends called her "the one who limps." She was missing an inch of bone in her hip, which caused her to walk slowly and with a limp. As if that were not enough, she was also missing a portion of muscle around the same area. God was greatly glorified on that day because He filled her hip with muscle and created the bone she had been missing. Suddenly, the woman was walking around and even jumping without the hint of a limp. She was moving so fast, it looked as if she were late for some important appointment. She could not stop giving thanks to the Lord. God did it again!

Remember, the act of thanksgiving establishes a foundation on which to build the throne of praise and worship. Praise is the attitude and action of proclaiming the powerful deeds that God has done. Worship declares who He is. Together, they involve the body, soul, and spirit. When the throne of God is built, the atmosphere will be ready to declare what He is saying and doing at that specific time. The powerful principles on which we build the throne and flow in God's supernatural power are generated from the priesthood at the altar and put into effect by leadership under His power and anointing. There are, however, other principles that affect those who will receive miracles.

6. Know the law of response.

Many Christians have seen excesses and abuses committed by those claiming to walk in the supernatural and have therefore rejected it completely. We must learn to respond to supernatural power without fear and skepticism. When we respond to authentic manifestations of the supernatural, we reap the kinds of victories and blessings that elude those who respond in error. Sometimes, Christians try to seek neutral ground on which they can continue to believe in God without having to risk taking a step of faith. They fail to see that this makes them useless to God and unable to bless other people. Furthermore, this type of Christian represents no threat to the enemy. Today, some preachers work hard to induce their people to respond to what God is doing. Still others have no idea how to do this, or even that they should do it. Some religious folks resist the miraculous because they think it has to do with the emotions exclusively.

We cannot stand rigidly by, doing nothing. We must praise and worship God. He wants to be celebrated, not tolerated. God must be loved, His glory yearned for, and His power perceived.

> ## *We will be judged for our lack of response when we are in God's presence and power.*

In some churches, God's presence can be felt, but nothing more happens. His presence is there because some people pray and fast, but no one knows how to respond or how to act when confronted with it. The atmosphere remains charged, yet nothing comes from it. This means the miracles, signs, wonders, deliverances, and transformations are stuck because people have no idea how to respond and appropriate these blessings.

How Does the Law of Response Operate?

And the power of the Lord was present to heal them.

(Luke 5:17)

In Luke 5, a multitude of people had gathered and were ready *"to be healed by Him of their infirmities"* (verse 15). In other words, the atmosphere was ready to produce miracles. Still, nothing happened. Perhaps they were waiting for Jesus to lay hands on them or to call them by name. Someone had to take hold of the supernatural. Soon, an individual who arrived late made his way in and, by force, took his miracle from the supernatural atmosphere that had been created by Jesus' prayer life. This bedridden man was lowered down to Jesus from a hole in the roof of the house! Luke wrote that *"the power of the Lord was present to heal them."* The power of God meets every need, and His grace encompasses all things—healing, deliverance, and so forth. It is necessary, however, that we respond like the man in Luke 5, or God's power will depart.

The realm of God's power that does not find a response does not remain.

In some churches, there are believers who used to know how to respond to God's power but then became too religious. They used to freely yell and dance during worship, but now they think of themselves as being too dignified for that kind of thing. This is partly why God allows (rather than causes) pain in our lives. When it hurts, we have no choice but to cry out, forgetting our reputations or what others might think, and praise Him wholeheartedly. Many people who have suffered much praise God continuously. I challenge us to respond right now! God is loosening His power for healing and deliverance. I challenge us to give a shout of victory and proclaim ourselves to be healed and free. I declare that a creative miracle is taking place in our bodies right now. But we must respond!

The manifestation of the power of God to which we respond is the only one that remains.

God's power is present; it waits only for us to respond, regardless of what we need—physical healing or a creative miracle, such as a new bone, an internal organ, eyesight, hair growth, muscle growth, or anything else. Now is the time to receive it. Those who have faith to act, do it now!

God's power is always present but is not always received.

We can preach a powerful revelation, but nothing will happen if people don't respond. Where there is freedom, the Holy Spirit can perform miracles, but if nothing happens, people will remain in bondage. God loves spontaneity. Anything else is just a mechanical, empty response. Feel free to praise, worship, dance, shout, and respond in ways that you have never responded before. Remember, we are responding to God's anointing and glory.

I encourage you to begin doing what you could not do before. As you do it, I declare you healed and free. I declare that, even now, creative miracles are being produced in your body, and supernatural manifestations of God are taking place in your mind and heart. I pray that as you read this chapter, you will begin to react, respond, and receive your miracle. Declare it with your mouth. Begin to praise and worship God and make a corresponding action to your need. Then, thank Him in the name of Jesus. Amen!

I want our faith to rise to another level. Here is another testimony that proclaims that God is ready to heal:

During a healing service, a woman from Santo Domingo, Dominican Republic, came to the altar to testify. As the result of a terrible car accident, she had been in a wheelchair for twelve years, and she could not move. But when the power of God descended upon her, she was suddenly able to do all of the things she had not been able to do before. Now, she was able to move, walk, jump, bend over, and even run without pain. This woman was overjoyed. She could not believe what had happened to her, and she never stopped giving thanks to God. What had happened? The woman responded to the glory of God in our presence, and she took hold of her miracle. She made a corresponding action by immediately testifying to her healing. Will you follow her example?

7. Understand the law of expectation.

So he gave them his attention, expecting to receive something from them.
(Acts 3:5)

Faith manifests what was already predetermined; therefore, there is expectancy for something to happen.

When people visit our church for the first time, they typically have not experienced the supernatural and do not come with the faith to believe for a miracle. I cannot lay hands on people who do not expect anything to happen. In some cases, they become offended at this, but no one can give them what they are not ready to receive. As believers, we must always expect to receive a miracle, healing, deliverance, or some other supernatural event. In some cases, people sing worship songs that actually destroy their faith—songs that highlight their pain instead of declaring the healing that God has already provided for them. There are even some preachers who struggle to help their own congregations receive miracles because they themselves lack genuine expectancy. I have noticed that the level of expectancy generated by guest preachers is not the same as that generated by the local preacher.

I believe that God is loosening a supernatural expectancy in all believers. When He does, regardless of who is preaching, people will be able to come and take their miracles from the eternal realm. Can you imagine the entire body of Christ expecting something from God? In those days, even if you don't have the gift of healing, the expectancy from the people of God will cause His power to manifest.

> *The secret to flowing in miracles is knowing God's time to manifest them and always expecting something to happen.*

Here is an example of how God works miracles when people have expectancy:

I was once in Peru preaching to two thousand pastors and leaders. The level of expectancy was great. They welcomed me as a man of God and accepted my message as God's word. Their expectancy placed a great demand on the mantle God had put on me. In the crowd was a woman on a stretcher with an illness that affected her back, keeping her from making even the slightest movement. As I preached, this woman placed a demand, or expectancy, on my mantle. Soon, she stood, grabbed her blankets, and came down to the altar to testify that God had healed her. The next day, she returned with her family and with medical documentation confirming her previous medical condition and the fact that God had healed her. Another woman in the crowd testified that God had created five new gold teeth in her mouth. Dozens of other miracles also took place because the people placed a demand upon my anointing and their level of expectancy was great.

8. Declare the Word with conviction that the words you speak will come to pass.

We cannot declare the Word of God without having foreknowledge of what will happen. If we don't want something to happen, we shouldn't declare anything. If we are going to speak to a blind person but don't expect his sight to return, we shouldn't say anything. If we tell the lame to stand up, but we have no expectation that anything will happen, we shouldn't speak. If we speak to a deaf-mute and fully expect that he will hear and speak, then we must speak, declare, and wait for him to hear and speak. There should be no doubt in our minds that the words we speak will do what they were sent to do. If we have the smallest doubt about something happening, we have not yet overcome the limitations of our faith. We are still in bondage to time, matter, and space. We cannot speak to matter until we have control and dominion over it. Do we now understand why intellectual knowledge is worthless when it comes to spiritual matters? To move in the supernatural, we must go beyond the natural, material realm. We must begin to exercise dominion over the laws of nature.

Don't speak the Word if you doubt that anything will happen.

By the word of the LORD the heavens were made, and all the host of them by the breath of His mouth. (Psalm 33:6)

When God's Word is spoken, and it joins with the breath of the Holy Spirit, it produces an explosion called "creative power" and is confirmed by the Holy Spirit. This divine, supernatural power will make the blind see, the deaf hear, the mute speak, and the lame walk—God still performs creative miracles. If we speak like God, with the intent to see something happen, there is no alternative: something will happen. It can be declared without any margin of error.

...upholding all things by the word of His power.
(Hebrews 1:3)

Confession is speaking what God has said; rhema is speaking what God is saying now.

God's Word will come to pass. Here is a testimony that demonstrates this truth:

During a healing conference in Mexico, a thirteen-year-old who had been missing two toes since birth came forward. He was poor and had sold pastries in the street in order to earn money to attend the conference, where his determination to receive a miracle paid off. When God's glory manifested, a wave of creative miracles began to take place. I instructed the people to check themselves to see whether or not any conditions they'd had were healed. This young boy hurriedly took off his socks and, to his surprise, saw two new toes on the foot that had been missing them for years. God did a creative, visible, tangible miracle in that young man's life. He was so ecstatic with joy that he could not stop smiling.

The problem with many of today's churches is that too many Christians believe based on only their own abilities. If what they see or hear doesn't fit with what they consider normal, it is rejected. Few dare to go beyond the natural. Instead, they prefer to stay comfortable in a church where nothing happens because they fear making mistakes or looking foolish. The vast majority of believers don't attend church expecting to see something supernatural take place. If anything supernatural does occur, they are shocked and amazed. I have to ask: If we don't expect God to manifest, why go to church at all?

To activate God's supernatural power, we must be able to respond to the atmosphere generated by prayer, praise, and worship. To do this, we need to expect something supernatural to happen. If we expect nothing, we will be unable to respond when there is a manifestation of God's power to create miracles. God is extending His hand to give us the supernatural, but we have to extend our hands to receive it.

In conclusion, we have learned many principles and concepts related to flowing in the supernatural, including prayer, intercession, revelation, praise, worship, atmosphere, the laws of reaction and expectancy, and speaking the creative word. All of these things work together to enable God's glory to manifest in order to heal the sick, deliver the captives, and proclaim the gospel of Jesus throughout the earth so that His name may be glorified. This is how the world will know and be able to experience our supernatural God.

Today, my dear friend, you can do this, too. All you have to do is respond to the things you have read with expectancy, believing that the God who moved in the Bible and in my life will also move in your life.

Summary

- Praise is proclaiming God's powerful deeds, while worship is prostrating or bowing down before His presence with reverence and humility.

- Thanksgiving, praise, and worship build a throne on which God can sit in our presence.

- Praise and worship are the elements most closely connected to the manifestation of God's glory because they incite Him to reveal Himself. They are genuine expressions in which we lose all awareness of self and focus only on Him.

- Praise reveals God's presence. The level of worship we reach will determine the type of miracles we experience.

- A supernatural atmosphere is built through a life of personal, collective, conscious, and constant prayer.

- When it comes to spiritual atmosphere, we must discern it, loosen whatever exists within it, and expect to receive from it.

10

Jesus Manifesting His Supernatural Power through the Believer

The book of Acts marks the end of Jesus' ministry on earth and the beginning of the ministry of His church. The first five chapters can be viewed as a bridge that leads to a new stage. From that point forward, we are the ones who continue the work that Jesus started. We were birthed to continue doing what He began. This is why He empowered us with the same power and authority He had received from the Father, so that everyone who believes in that power can access it and do the same works as Jesus. The book of Acts records the many miraculous works performed by the apostles as they were led by the Holy Spirit, but it also opens the way for every believer to participate in the personal victories God gives to him as he obeys in the name of Jesus.

An *act* refers to actions, works, or events. It is something we do, such as preaching the Word with demonstrations of God's supernatural power to heal and perform miracles. It also incorporates the progress of the fulfillment of the Great Commission. In the same way, you and I should be able to write accounts of the works of the Holy Spirit performed through our lives. The first apostles seemed to be working constantly. They healed the sick, rebuked demons, and performed miracles. They shouldered the responsibility of advancing the kingdom of God. They formed the first church. Believe it or not, Jesus mentioned the church considerably less than He did the kingdom. From the onset of His ministry until His resurrection, Jesus prioritized the kingdom of God. The church is the growing manifestation of God's kingdom that serves Jesus, but the kingdom is greater than the church.

What Names Are Given to the Church in Scripture?

In the Bible, God's people are referred to by different names: church, body, work, temple, family, bride, and army. Some say the church is like a hospital, but the Bible never refers to it by this term. Yes, the church restores and heals the sick, the fallen, the sad, and the depressed, but this is not its most important function.

What Is the Church?

The church is the body of Christ. The Greek word for "church" is *ekklesia*, which means "a gathering of citizens called out from their homes into some public place...for the purpose of deliberating." The origin of this word is found in two Hebrew terms: *edah*, meaning "divine testimonies," and *qahal*, meaning "to assemble, gather...for religious reasons." *Ekklesia* has two characteristics: first, there is a *calling* of individuals to gather together; second, there is a *purpose* for the calling. In short, *ekklesia* is a group of people called to gather for a specific purpose. For the church, we are called by Jesus for the purpose of carrying out His will on earth.

In other words, we were called out of the world to form the body of Christ and to obey Jesus, its Head. However, the Head can do nothing unless the body is willing to move. If my head wants to go through a doorway, it makes the decision, and the body must obey and move. If I want to pick up something from the floor, the head will decide before the hand stretches to perform the corresponding action. Likewise, Jesus—as the Head—has plans, desires, a purpose, a mission, and a mandate, but these cannot be carried out unless the body obeys. In my case, even if my head wanted to leave my body behind and carry out the plan on its own, it couldn't because the function of the head is to command, and the function of the body is to execute, or carry out, that command.

When God tells us to do something, it is because He is not going to do it for us.

For example, God told us to proclaim the gospel of the kingdom throughout the world, beginning in our homes, neighborhoods, cities, and nations, but He also told us to make disciples, heal the sick, and cast out demons. If we would obey, He promised that signs would follow. (See Mark 16:20.)

> *And I also say to you that you are Peter, and on this rock I will build My church, and the gates of Hades shall not prevail against it.* (Matthew 16:18)

Jesus did not delegate the task of the building of His church to anyone. He did it Himself, founded on the revelation, or revealed knowledge, that He was the Messiah, the Lord of Lords and King of Kings.

Ekklesia was also used to designate the state governmental body, which, in Greece, was led by its male citizens. For Christians, the church comprises people around the world who are called to establish a kingdom government and authority on earth by proclaiming the gospel of Jesus Christ with signs and miracles. Unfortunately, today, there is insufficient evidence of God's kingdom government on earth because we have failed to fully exercise our responsibility as administrators of His government.

As the church, we are even responsible for many bad things taking place because we have not used our delegated authority to declare them illegal. If we want to change the nation, we must begin by changing the church. Are we aware of our responsibilities? In Rome, once a law was passed, it could not be challenged. Local officials, however, could issue decrees over the areas they ruled. Similarly, Jesus created our laws, and they cannot be challenged. But we can make decrees.

> *Whatever you bind (declare to be improper and unlawful) on earth must be what is already bound in heaven; and whatever you loose (declare lawful) on earth must be what is already loosed in heaven.* (Matthew 16:19 AMP)

We must learn to speak new decrees in order to make the laws of the kingdom come to pass on earth. Jesus carries out His eternal goals through the church, regardless of how long it takes. In fact, it has taken twenty centuries to carry the gospel to the nations, and we still have not finished reaching the last corners of the earth. We must flood the nations with miracles, signs, and wonders. Jesus will not do the job that we were entrusted with. Many believers lack supernatural authority because they have not learned to walk under supernatural authority. Some are rebellious and must learn to submit to the Head: Jesus.

Anything not subject to the Head is not the body, or the church.

What Are the Goals of the Church?

1. To proclaim the gospel of the kingdom throughout the world

> *And this gospel of the kingdom will be preached in all the world as a witness to all the nations, and then the end will come.* (Matthew 24:14)

Believers are supposed to be the salt of the earth and the light of the world (see Matthew 5:13–14), ambassadors, fishers of men, armor bearers, witnesses, kings, priests, representatives of

Jesus, and peacemakers. In essence, we are to be "little Christs." We have a mission and a mandate: to preach the gospel to every creature with miracles, signs, wonders, and demonstrations of God's power that confirm we are an extension of Jesus on earth. God continues calling people to go and carry out this mandate.

2. To make disciples of all nations

Go therefore and make disciples of all the nations.
(Matthew 28:19)

In our church, we have thousands of disciples, both in the United States and throughout twenty-five other nations. Each disciple is being trained and equipped to heal the sick, preach the gospel of the kingdom, and perform miracles, signs, and wonders in his neighborhood, territory, and city of the world.

3. To manifest the life of the kingdom

That the life of Jesus also may be manifested in our mortal flesh. *(2 Corinthians 4:11)*

The life of the kingdom is the resurrected life of Jesus, which has been made available, by faith, to every believer. The life of Jesus is made manifest in our mortal bodies. It is what I call "divine health and healing." If we have it, then we can also minister that life of resurrection to others to heal and deliver them. Many believers are incapable of manifesting the eternal, or resurrected, life of Jesus because they have yet to "die to self." That means dying to the soul-led, emotional life and instead choosing to live a Spirit-led life. In order to manifest the life of Jesus, this is the only requirement.

Unless a grain of wheat falls into the ground and dies, it remains alone; but if it dies, it produces much grain.
(John 12:24)

Before Jesus went to the cross, He gave His disciples a kingdom principle that would guarantee their success and manifest the life of God: If you plant a seed, it will die; however, when the seed dies, it will reproduce a hundred times over. The plant that grows out of the dead seed will be the same as the seed because it has the seed's DNA. Until that moment, Jesus had been unable to reproduce His life in the lives of His disciples. To do that, He had to go to the cross to die for the sins of humanity and to redeem us. His sacrifice also made available the seed that, when planted in the spiritual womb of a believer, could reproduce its exact genetic components. Because of that seed, we can reach the measure of the perfect Man—Jesus.

The pattern of God includes planting a seed in our spirits that will grow and become like Jesus. This is known as the new birth. Jesus had to die to deposit that seed. Likewise, we must die so that our seed can produce abundant fruit, and so that the resurrected life of Christ can powerfully manifest and touch thousands who are suffering and in need. Ours will not be a physical death, however, but a spiritual one. If we want to minister that life to others, we must die to self—to our fleshly needs and desires, and to our emotional will—only this will open the door that allows Jesus to manifest.

Believers who manifest the life of the kingdom experience death to self.

4. To manifest the authority and power of the kingdom

Behold, I give you the authority to trample on serpents and scorpions, and over all the power of the enemy, and nothing shall by any means hurt you. (Luke 10:19)

The authority of the kingdom gives legal right to exercise God's power.

As previously stated, power is the ability to carry out something to completion. Authority is the legal right to exercise that power. To better illustrate this, imagine that a police officer orders a driver to pull over. If the driver has good judgment, he will stop out of respect for the uniform, the weapon, and the government the officer represents. If the driver is drunk, however, and his judgment is impaired, he might try to flee in an effort to avoid a ticket. In this case, the officer has the authority to order him to stop but not the physical power to make him stop. What would happen if the officer called for backup and a military tank were sent to his aid? Even a drunk driver would probably think twice before challenging a tank. Now, the officer would have both the authority *and* the power to stop the driver.

This is relevant to our spiritual condition in the spirit realm. God gave us His power when He sent His Holy Spirit the day we recognized Jesus as the Lord of our lives. God gave us His authority when He paid the wages of our sins at the cross. At that moment, Jesus made us coheirs with Him. In other words, the day we were born again, we also became God's children, with the authority, power, and legal right to exercise divine power in order to manifest the kingdom and carry out the mission Jesus commanded us to do.

5. To expand the kingdom of God

At the onset of creation, God created man to govern and exercise dominion and lordship over the earth. We—the believers—are the only instruments God uses to carry out His will and to expand His dominion upon the face of the earth, which we accomplish by proclaiming and demonstrating God's kingdom.

6. To proclaim the kingdom *without* visible demonstrations

John performed no sign, but all the things that John spoke about this Man were true. (John 10:41)

John the Baptist preached about the coming of Jesus, but he was not able to manifest any miraculous signs of the kingdom. Likewise, today, some men and women of God preach the truth and have the right doctrine but also are unable to demonstrate the supernatural power of God with miracles and signs because teaching, proclaiming, and announcing the kingdom through words alone is only the first phase. The true manifestation comes with Jesus.

7. To preach the kingdom *with* visible demonstrations of power

But if I cast out demons by the Spirit of God, surely the kingdom of God has come upon you. (Matthew 12:28)

When John the Baptist ended his ministry of announcing God's kingdom, a new phase began: the preaching phase. Jesus began this phase by preaching, teaching, and demonstrating the kingdom with miracles, signs and wonders, and by casting out demons. This was a new, unique occurrence. Never before had someone come to the Jews with the authority to cast out demons from the bodies and minds of people. Starting with Jesus, God's kingdom began to expand via the visible manifestations of God's power.

The casting out of demons is a visible sign that the kingdom has arrived.

The following testimony illustrates how the coming of God's kingdom can make demons flee at the mention of the name of Jesus:

A young woman who had been diagnosed with bipolar disorder, schizophrenia, and ADHD visited our church. This woman suffered from hallucinations, catatonic behavior, irrational behavior, and the imagining of strange voices in her head. She was chronically angry, anxious, and paranoid. Doctors had declared that she would most likely never be able to raise a family, drive a car, or function without the aid of prescribed medication.

Her condition had started when she was only eight years old. She thought that she heard a voice laughing and became so frightened that she went to her room and stayed there, unable to sleep, for a week. By the age of twelve, she was institutionalized in a psychiatric hospital, where she was sedated twenty-four hours a day. She was taking up to fifteen pills each day and had tried to commit suicide several times. She claimed that she could see demons tormenting her and threatening to kill her family. Whenever she was able to leave the hospital, she would escape to a park, where she would spend the night getting high on illegal drugs. She hated the world and was angry at everything and everyone around her.

On the day when a fellow student invited her to church, she received the Lord. The following Sunday, the Holy Spirit led me to where she was sitting, and I prayed for her, rebuking all the demons that tormented her life. That day, she became free. As soon as she got home, she threw away all of her pills. Her mother was initially angry at the church, but her daughter kept insisting that she was healed. A few days later, her mother took her to the doctor, who confirmed that she was free indeed! Today, this woman, her mother, and the rest of her family attend our church and serve God.

8. To advance the kingdom of God by force

And from the days of John the Baptist until now the kingdom of heaven suffers violence, and the violent take it by force. (Matthew 11:12)

A more literal translation of this verse would read, "From the days of John the Baptist until now, the kingdom of God has been governed by force, and only those with power control it." This is the violent phase of our spiritual war—the conflict between the kingdom of God and the kingdom of darkness. In this phase, we preach and teach, establishing and extending God's divine government over new territories. With each step we take, we remove, cast out, and uproot the enemy from his territory, causing a violent collision between the two kingdoms.

The Church Cooperates with God in the Expansion of the Kingdom

For we are God's fellow workers. (1 Corinthians 3:9)

As we learn of the responsibilities and purpose of the church, we realize that we have failed Jesus. He called us to be His associates—His collaborators and representatives on earth—because He decided not to do anything except through us, the church.

What Channel Does Jesus Use to Operate on Earth?

Our physical bodies are the instruments Jesus uses to operate on earth. All of His plans will be carried out by His body, the church.

We are the extension of Jesus. Through our bodies, He touches the world.

As the body of Christ, we are the only ones capable of putting limits on what Jesus can do on earth. God will not do more than what His body asks or allows—not because He can't or doesn't want to but because He has delegated His gospel, authority, and power to His body. Furthermore, since the kingdom is within us, this makes us extremely valuable. What requirement must be fulfilled in order to operate as His body? The requirement of interdependence. Each member of the body needs the others, and yet, not one member is indispensable. The purpose of the body—the church—is to be used by Jesus to manifest the supernatural in the natural realm of space, time, and matter. He depends on us in order to operate in this dimension. When Jesus came to earth, He Himself needed a body to carry out His Father's will. The same is true today. After Jesus' departure, the body of Christ became the instrument He used to continue His ministry and establish His will in this world.

Jesus paved a new way that allows everyone to enter into His presence and to know Him personally. He did not create a religion based on rituals, which are the antithesis of miracles. Our mission is to share His life and love with the world. God is love, and He loves us! If we love Him, then we will also love other people. How? By serving, praying, and ministering God's love, and by becoming channels through which Jesus can perform His miracles as a way of validating our message.

The Relationship between the Head and the Body of Christ

And the eye cannot say to the hand, "I have no need of you"; nor again the head to the feet, "I have no need of you."   (1 Corinthians 12:21)

Christ is the Head, and, as such, He cannot tell the hands or feet, "I don't need you." What the Head requires of the feet is the availability and willingness to carry out its decisions. Regardless of how talented I might be as a Christian, if I am not available and willing to submit to the Head—Jesus—I am worthless for the kingdom. Christ will use His body to destroy the works of Satan: sickness, oppression, and captivity.

Once, when I was on my way out of a service, exhausted and ready to go directly home, a young woman approached and asked me to pray for healing. She had been deaf from birth. Although I was exhausted, I felt the demand of God and His compassion asking me to lend Him my humanity. I didn't even lay hands on her. As I spoke, the power of God fell, and she was instantly healed. From this experience, I was able to conclude that regardless of how tired we might be, it is wonderful to surrender our bodies to the Holy Spirit so that He can use them to bless others.

For What Divine Reasons Did God Give Us Bodies?

The main reason God gave us bodies was to make us His habitation and to place His glory within us. God does not live in man-made temples. The temple He designed is your body and mine, and that is where He wants to live.

> *Behold, the tabernacle of God is with men, and He will dwell with them, and they shall be His people. God Himself will be with them and be their God.* (Revelation 21:3)

God will not dwell permanently in a man-made temple. He will make His habitation in the temple of His doing.

What Type of Dwelling Place Is God Looking For?

> *You also, as living stones, are being built up a spiritual house, a holy priesthood.* (1 Peter 2:5)

After many years and a huge amount of money, Solomon's temple was finally completed. It was an amazing structure. It did not last, though, because it was destroyed as a result of the sin of Israel. God decided not to continue investing in stone and mortar but in the dust of the earth. With the coming of Christ, we became His temple. He could not have worked with more valuable materials, as we were purchased with blood— the blood of His precious Son, Jesus.

> *That the world may know that You have sent Me, and have loved them as You have loved Me.* (John 17:23)

Therefore, as believers, we no longer belong to the devil; we belong to God. Why is God looking for a dwelling place? Because this gives Him the legal right to operate on earth and perform supernatural signs and wonders. Is there a better reason than that to glorify Him through our lives? Let us surrender our bodies to Him!

How Does Jesus Minister Today?

Christ in you, the hope of glory.　　　　　(Colossians 1:27)

Jesus ministers today in the same way He did over two thousand years ago: by using our bodies. We are His collaborators, associates, friends, ambassadors, interpreters, witnesses, and communicators. We carry His message of love, power, glory, and authority. Unfortunately, many believers have abandoned their responsibilities. Many are willing to pay for others to do them because they don't want to themselves. The revelation of this mystery is that Jesus lives in you and wants to minister through you. He needs us to lend Him our bodies so that He can reach our families and friends.

Jesus redeemed us so that He could live and express Himself through us, the believers.

God's power to heal and deliver has been given to all believers, as seen in this testimony:

During a Sunday service at our church, I declared that everyone who had come with sickness, or with any other problem, would not return home in the same condition. A House of Peace leader who had been attending our church for only a few months and was already trained to walk in the supernatural appropriated that word. At the end of the service, she encountered a man from the Dominican Republic who was completely bald. She approached him in a very gentle way and asked if it was all right for her to pray for him. He accepted her request, and, in one of the hallways of the church, in front of many witnesses, she placed her hands on his head and prayed. Immediately, all who were present witnessed the miracle of his hair growing before their own eyes.

By myself, I cannot heal anyone. Jesus is the only One who heals. This is the mystery: Jesus came, died, was resurrected, received all power and authority, and then delegated that power to us. Why didn't God send His angels to do the job? Because the angels were not redeemed. We are the only beings for whom Jesus died. If we don't take our responsibility seriously, many will be lost!

Preaching the gospel is limited by man's will to obey what God commanded him to do.

Jesus can visit a sick person or a prisoner using our bodies. He will go in us and with us. He cannot do it any other way. Unfortunately, many people use prayer as an excuse not to go. Please, don't misunderstand. Jesus prayed because it is important to do so, but in many cases, He also *went* to pray for them while He was in a human body.

> *God anointed Jesus of Nazareth with the Holy Spirit and with power, who went about doing good and healing all who were oppressed by the devil, for God was with Him.*
> (Acts 10:38)

As He went, Jesus testified, healed, preached, rebuked demons, declared and demonstrated God's compassion, and put His words into action. Do we want God to do our part, too? He will not do it! We have to do the possible, and then, He will do the impossible. There are two types of prayer that God will never answer: when we ask Him to do what He has already done, and when we ask Him to do what we are supposed to do as His church. How will Jesus do His part? By using our lives. He will work in you, *"for it is God who works in you both to will and to do for His good pleasure"* (Philippians 2:13).

Likewise, Jesus can visit the needy and heal the broken-hearted and the depressed only through us. He encourages those in despair through us because we are His hands and feet. Therefore, if all we do is pray, but we never visit the lost or the sick, and we never testify of His love and saving grace, then we are not His body. We must pray, but we also must go and do.

People will never see Jesus except through us.

God Entrusted His Gospel to You and Me

The glorious gospel of the blessed God...was committed to my trust. (1 Timothy 1:11)

God ordained that His gospel should be entrusted to regular people like you and me. It is a great privilege to preach it. Jesus sat down in heaven because His job is done. He entrusted us with it in order to share it with the world.

Jesus in us gives us purpose.

What Must We Do?

Now that God has restored us and revealed His supernatural power, chosen and anointed us to go in His name, and made us His representatives, we must go. Now that we understand that,...

- each believer has the ability, power, and authority given by God to move in miracles, signs, and wonders;

- His supernatural power comes from the cross;

- the anointing is available to everyone;
- we must decide to go!

Jesus served the people, spoke what was needed, and ministered His love and compassion. He has not changed. The only difference between then and now is that now, He does it through you and me—but only if we allow Him to. How does this happen? The fullness of His power will be loosened if we meet these basic conditions:

- **Total commitment**

Surrender without reservation and present your body as a living sacrifice so your hands can become His hands, your feet can become His feet, and your mouth can become His mouth. Then, you can heal the sick, deliver the captives, save the lost, perform miracles, signs, and wonders, and manifest His glory everywhere.

- **Total obedience**

Everyone must decide to obey His Word and keep His mandate. We don't need further confirmation; the harvest is ready. People are alone, sick, and without God. They are hopeless and lost, crying out for help. As I said, all we have to do is go and gather the harvest.

- **Total availability**

We must be ready the moment the Lord wants to manifest His glory through us. As members of His body, we must always be ready, available, and willing to be used by the Head. Regardless of how strong a body part is, it is useless if it is not available to do what the Head wants it to do.

The only ability God seeks in mankind is availability.

The world is hurting, waiting for a special touch to rescue them from the emptiness of life. Remember that Jesus will continue His healing ministry through you, and you will continue to grow as you share Christ with others. As long as you allow

Him to use you as His instrument to bless others, you are His body, His temple. To be used by God to bless other people causes incredible joy and is at the heart of Christianity—*"Christ in you, the hope of glory"* (Colossians 1:27), to win souls, proclaim the gospel, and perform miracles, signs, and wonders.

We Were Chosen and Anointed for Action

We cannot learn to move in God's anointing if we are not guided by revealed knowledge. When knowledge is received and shared, enjoyed and given, heard and communicated, it becomes rooted within us—it becomes ours. Otherwise, it is like a dead tree, stagnant water, or dry seed. In Matthew 5–7, Jesus preached His Sermon at the Mount. But when Matthew 8 begins, we see Him perform miracles and demonstrate the things He taught. You would be surprised to see what could happen if you laid hands on the sick, declaring the Word that lives within you. People can be healed, free, and restored because we walk in the same anointing as Jesus did. Can we answer God's call, saying, as Isaiah did, *"Here am I! Send Me"* (Isaiah 6:8)? "Lord, I lend You my humanity of my own free will to speak to the lost, encourage the brokenhearted, heal the sick, and deliver the afflicted and those in mourning. Lord, I will serve You. Send me!" I ask you again, if God were to call you, would you answer Him this way?

This challenge comes from God to you. Repeat this prayer aloud:

> I am a believer—a Christian—and Jesus is my Lord. I believe that Jesus was raised from the dead. He guarantees His promises, and I will experience His supernatural power because Christ is resurrected in me. The Holy Spirit has anointed me with power from above to believe that all things are possible. Jesus is greater than any problem or challenge before me. He lives in me, and the power that raised Him from the dead is working in my life as I speak. Satan knows this and cannot do anything

about it. Jesus, You publicly humiliated the enemy and destroyed his works. Now, You live in me, giving me the grace to experience Your power, heal the sick, deliver the captives, perform miracles and marvels in Your name, and preach Your gospel throughout the nations. As long as there is breath within me, Lord, use me wherever I may go to continue Your ministry. Amen.

Once, I received a powerful miracle while in Mexico, during a crusade in the city of Villahermosa. A police officer who had been almost entirely paralyzed for one year had been brought to the crusade. He had been shot in the back, which had necessitated the removal of two discs. While we were praying, I asked those who were sick to repeat the following prayer: "Tonight is the night for my miracle." At that moment, this man appropriated the word and repeated it with all his might. Suddenly, he felt the right side of his body begin to tremble so much that he thought he was dying. When I ordered the lame to rise and walk, this man desperately began to look for someone to help him stand up. He called to his daughter, who was close by, but she was too afraid to help him. Not to be denied his miracle, the man used her for support, pushed himself up, and began to walk. After a few steps, he realized that he had been completely healed. Later, he even returned to his job as a police officer. His testimony has led more than sixty people to Christ, including the chief of police.

If you have never given your life to Jesus, I want to give you another opportunity to know the real, living, and resurrected Christ. This is the same prayer from the end of chapter four. If you believe that Jesus came to shed His blood so that you might live, please repeat this prayer:

Heavenly Father, I recognize that I am a sinner. I repent of all my sins. I confess with my mouth that Jesus is the Son of God and that the Father raised Him from the dead. I am saved, healed, and delivered. I am a son/daughter of God, created in His image, to manifest His person and His power on this earth. Amen!

About the Author

Apostle Guillermo Maldonado is a man called to establish the kingdom of God at the local and international level. He is the founder of King Jesus International Ministry—the fastest growing Hispanic church in the United States with services in both English and Spanish—recognized for its powerful manifestations of the Holy Spirit. Apostle Maldonado, having earned a master's degree in Practical Theology from Oral Roberts University and a doctorate in Divinity from Wagner Leadership Institute, stands firm and focused on the vision God has given him to evangelize, affirm, disciple, and send. His purpose is to encourage leaders to become true spiritual fathers, capable of leaving a legacy of blessings for future generations. This mission encompasses the United States, the Caribbean, Central America, South America, and Europe. Apostle Maldonado is a spiritual father to many leaders and apostles of local and international churches through those regions as part of The New Wine Apostolic Network, which he founded.

Apostle Maldonado resides in Miami, Florida, with his wife and partner in ministry, Ana, and their two sons, Bryan and Ronald.